KT-412-035

South Wales

MICHELIN
Travel Publications

CONTENTS

INTRODUCTION

■ Geography

The principality is approached from the east via the English **Marches**, attractive farming country interspersed with hill ranges anticipating the mountains beyond. In the south, marking the border near Chepstow, is the luxuriantly wooded gorge of the Wye. To the west lies Cardiff, the capital, flanked by the other former coal ports of the coast which were supplied by the immense coalfield of South Wales, a high plateau deeply cut by valleys filled with mining settlements. North of the mining country is the great bastion of the red sandstone escarpment of the **Brecon Beacons**. Further west the scene is rural, rolling country ending in the cliffs and rocks of the **Pembrokeshire Coast National Park**.

■ Historical notes

Prehistory: c 24000 BC to AD 78

Stone Age – The headless skeleton of a 25-year-old man provides the earliest evidence of human life in Wales. It was found in Paviland Cave, on the southern Gower Peninsula, where its ritual burial probably took place in about 24 000 BC.

Bronze Age – From about 1800 BC gold, copper and bronze work was introduced into Britain by the Beaker People, named for their practice of burying earthenware pots with their dead in single graves. Stone was still in wide use; during this period the bluestone slabs used to construct Stonehenge in Wiltshire were quarried in the Presely Hills of Pembrokeshire.

National Parks in South Wales

The first National Park was established in 1951 to preserve the distinctive characteristics of certain rural areas of England and Wales.

Pembrokeshire Coast – Second smallest of the Parks, for much of its length it is less than three miles wide. Steep cliffs display spectacularly folded and twisted rock formations, sheltered bays invite bathing and scuba-diving. Offshore islands such as Skomer and Skokholm support huge colonies of seabirds.

Brecon Beacons – High red sandstone mountains divide the ancient rocks of mid-Wales from the coalfields and industrialisation further south. Along the southern edge of the Park a limestone belt provides a dramatic change in scenery and there are hundreds of sink-holes and cave systems, the most spectacular being the Dan-yr-Ogof Caves at the head of the Tawe valley.

Celtic Tribes – The Celts first settled in Britain c 1000 BC, having spread from central Europe through the Mediterranean and into Asia Minor. While the Goidelic Celts inhabited Ireland, the Brittonic branch moved into England and Wales, bringing with them sophisticated bronze-working and farming skills. Modern Wales can trace its language and elements of its culture back to the Celtic age, which lasted well over a thousand years.

Wales under the Romans: AD 78 to 5C

Claudius, the Roman Emperor, successfully invaded Britain in AD 43 and by AD 76-78 the western Celtic tribes were under attack. Anglesey, headquarters of the Druids, was conquered in 78, despite the spirited resistance of painted women, who screamed at terrified troops across the Menai Strait. Military bases, linked by long roads, were set up in **Caernarfon** *(Segontium)*, **Chester** *(Deva)*, **Brecon** *(Y Gaer)* and **Caerleon** *(Isca)* to control western territory. On the whole, Celtic life continued undisturbed and many leading families were integrated into Roman society. Some British leaders, such as Magnus Maximus, known in Welsh as Macsen Wledig were even granted a measure of autonomy.

Post-Roman Invasions: 5C to 11C

As Roman troops began to withdraw in the 5C, Britain became the target of a series of new invaders. Goidels from Ireland and Picts from Scotland threat-

ened the British Celts from west and north, and Anglo-Saxons swept across the south and east. The Brythons, confined to the western mainland, now began to refer to themselves as *Cymry* (meaning

South Wales

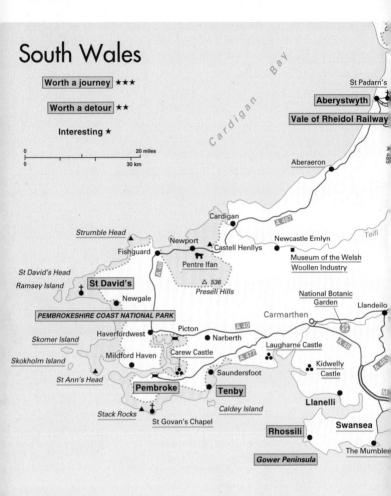

Worth a journey ★★★

Worth a detour ★★

Interesting ★

0 _____ 20 miles
0 _____ 30 km

Cardigan Bay

St Padarn's

Aberystwyth

Vale of Rheidol Railway

Aberaeron

Cardigan

Strumble Head

Newport

Fishguard

Newcastle Emlyn

Castell Henllys

Teifi

Museum of the Welsh
Woollen Industry

Pentre Ifan

St David's Head

Ramsey Island

St David's

Newgale

△ 536

Preseli Hills

National Botanic
Garden

Llandeilo

PEMBROKESHIRE COAST NATIONAL PARK

Picton

Carmarthen

Skomer Island

Haverfordwest

Narberth

Laugharne Castle

Skokholm Island

Mildford Haven

Carew Castle

Kidwelly
Castle

St Ann's Head

Saundersfoot

Pembroke

Tenby

Llanelli

Stack Rocks

St Govan's Chapel

Caldey Island

Rhossili

Swansea

The Mumbles

Gower Peninsula

BRISTOL   CHANNEL

"fellow countrymen") – still the Welsh name for its people; the Anglo-Saxons knew them as "We-leas", or "foreigners" or possibly "the Romanised people".

Missionaries – With the Irish invaders came Christian missionaries *(sancti)*. Previous attempts to convert the pagan Celts had met with little success: the Roman mis-

sionary, St Augustine, apparently offended local chiefs by remaining seated when they were presented to him. The *sancti* had more of an impact and were even granted parcels of land – the *llan* of many Welsh placenames – on which to establish a network of churches and monasteries. One of their number, born in Pembrokeshire in the mid-5C, became the patron saint of Wales, **David**, *Dewi* in Welsh.

Welsh Kings – During the 5C a powerful dynasty was established by Cunedda Wledig in north and west Wales, while other royal houses, possibly of Irish descent, emerged in the southwest. Wales was divided into several principalities, including Gwynedd, Powys, Meirionydd, Ceredigion, Dyfed and Gwent. Each one was a separate political unit, though on the whole they coexisted peacefully. Unity came only with the new threat of the Vikings, the Norsemen, who began their attacks on Britain in the late 8C. By this time three Anglo-Saxon kingdoms had evolved: Wessex in the south, Mercia in the midlands and Northumbria in the north. In 784 Offa, King of Mercia, marked the boundary between his territories and those of the Welsh with a ditch, **Offa's Dyke** (167mi/269km long), which still more or less defines the English-Welsh border.

By the 9C the Vikings had settled in northern Britain and Ireland and on the Isle of Man but they were kept out of Wales by **Rhodri Mawr**, Prince of Powys, who extended his rule through marriage to take In most of the Welsh lands. Nevertheless, while the Anglian (English) kingdoms of the east were developing into a single political power during the 9C and 10C, Wales could not sustain a unified system. The Welsh practice of gavelkind (*cyfran*) – sharing territory between all sons – ensured the division of Rhodri's inheritance into six princedoms, all of which submitted to Alfred, the English king.

Deheubarth — Rhodri Mawr's grandson, **Hywel Dda** (Hywel the Good) built up a new empire, uniting the southern territories into the Kingdom of Deheubarth (south-west Wales) and extending his rule to Gwynedd and Powys. He advocated the policy of living at peace with the English and of paying tribute to the men of Wessex. He too, however, was forced to accept the supremacy of the English throne; he died in 950. His main achievement was to collect and codify the laws and customs of Wales to form a legal system which lasted until the 13C.

Normans and Welsh Uprisings: 1066 to 1485

Hywel Dda's death was followed by a return to confusion and sporadic internal warfare, leaving the country vulnerable to Norman incursions. William of Normandy, having led his troops to victory against King Harold in 1066, rewarded his closest associates with lands along the Marches (borders) of Wales. The Marcher lords made several inroads into Welsh territory and by the 12C Powys and Gwynedd were cut off from much of the rest of Wales. Norman gains were consolidated with motte-and-bailey castles, first of earth and timber, later rebuilt in stone.

Tudors: 1485 to 1603

During the 15C England was torn apart by the Wars of the Roses, a power struggle between the royal houses of Lancaster and York. In 1471 the Lancastrian king Henry VI was murdered and the throne passed to the Yorkists. The Welsh **Tudor** *(Tewdwr)* family had become deeply embroiled in the feud. Lancastrian Henry V's widow, Catherine de Valois, had married Owain Tewdwr of Anglesey,

Tintern Abbey, Monmouthshire

and their grandson, Henry, now became the Lancastrian claimant. After 14 years in exile in Brittany he returned in 1485, hailed by the Welsh as the new leader prophesied by their bards, and defeated Richard III at Bosworth. As Henry VII he ended the civil war by marrying Elizabeth of York and uniting the two houses, and founded the Tudor dynasty that would rule for another 118 years.

Acts of Union – Henry's son, Henry VIII, was determined to introduce a uniform political and judicial structure throughout England and Wales. His Acts of Union (1536 and 1543) abolished the Marcher lordships and allowed Welshmen full inheritance rights. A standardised English system of law courts was established and the Welsh language was excluded from all official channels. While covering the Welsh by the same law as the rest of the kingdom, the Acts created an even deeper gulf between the Anglicised gentry and the largely illiterate, Welsh-speaking lower classes. The survival of the language was in great part due to the growing influence of the church and to the publication of a Bible translated into Welsh by **William Morgan** in 1588.

Social and Industrial Development: 17C to 19C

Religion and Reformation – Henry VIII's creation of a Protestant, Anglican church, headed by the king, met with no real opposition in Wales but by the late 17C there was considerable dissatisfaction with church authorities. Most clergymen were badly educated and badly paid; many bishops were non-resident and none spoke Welsh. In the 1730s **Gruffydd Jones** of Llanddowror (1683-1761) set out to reach the illiterate populace through his system of circulating schools, teaching adults and children to read the Bible in Welsh. The bid to win congregations with education was continued by **Thomas Charles** of Bala (1755-1814), who organised Sunday schools and founded the British and Foreign Bible Society, providing cheap Bibles. **Methodism**, which had started as an unconventional movement within the Anglican church, received fervent support in Wales, where it was led by **Howel Harris** of Trefeca (1714-73) and **Daniel Rowland** of Llangeitho (1713-90), both highly emotional, charismatic preachers. In 1811 the Methodists left the Anglican church and for the following 150 years its various Nonconformist offshoots continued to wield a strong influence among the Welsh.

Industrialisation – From the late 18C, industrialists began serious exploitation of the mineral wealth of Wales. Slate quarries, copper mines and smelting works appeared in the north and the south, and industrial activity gathered pace during the iron boom of the early 19C. By 1827 Wales was producing half of Britain's iron exports.

Coal, originally mined for iron-smelting, was also in increasing demand, to fire steam trains and ships and to provide domestic fuel. A series of mines sunk in the South Wales valleys transformed the landscape: houses were thrown up in long terraces, eventually to be overshadowed by black slag-heaps. Despite appalling conditions, people flocked to the valleys to find work in the mines and to escape from rural poverty. Close communities were created, with the coal pits as their focus, and the valley towns became the breeding ground for a radical political culture.

Industrial barons reaped vast profits from advances in technology and transport. Railways carried coal from the valleys to new docks built by the Second Marquess of Bute at Cardiff, which grew to be the biggest coal-shipping port in the world. While coal and slate masters flourished, building extravagant homes such as **Cardiff Castle** and **Penrhyn Castle**, their workers lived on low wages, in dangerous and insanitary conditions. Riots were not uncommon: 20 people were killed in the Merthyr Riots of 1831; 28 died in Newport in 1839 during demonstrations in support of the Chartist movement for electoral and social reform.

Agricultural workers also suffered extreme hardship, exacerbated by depopulation and the imposition of toll charges on roads, discouraging itinerant trade. In the 1840s a spate of attacks on tollgates and houses was carried out by the so-called **Rebecca Rioters** – men dressed in women's clothes who usually operated under cover of night.

Politics and Education: 1800 to 1920

Political dissent and religious Nonconformity in Wales in the 19C were closely linked in opposition to the Anglican, mainly conservative landowners. Under the 1867 Reform Act industrial workers and tenant farmers were granted the right to vote and returned 23 Liberal members of parliament out of 33 in the 1868 elections. There followed a series of evictions from Tory-owned land which helped speed the introduction of the Secret Ballot Act (1872).

Wales remained predominantly Liberal until the 1920s, its most famous parliamentary representative being **David Lloyd George** (1863-1945), the member for Caernarfon Boroughs. As Chancellor of the Exchequer Lloyd George introduced a programme of social reform, which included the introduction of state pensions, and as Prime Minister he led the government during the First World War.

Disestablishment – By the late 19C the Anglican church had become an alien institution to the largely Nonconformist population of Wales. Resentment was particularly focused on the continuing obligation to pay tithes, an ancient Anglican tax. Strength of feeling was such that several violent riots broke out in North Wales, and the growing calls for change eventually led, after several false starts, to the passing of a Disestablishment Bill through parliament in 1914. In 1920 the Anglican church in Wales was disendowed and its money passed to the University, the National Library and Welsh county councils.

Schools and the Welsh language – Education in the 18C and the 19C was largely in the hands of the Nonconformist churches. In 1846 three English lawyers were sent as part of a government commission to assess Welsh schools. Their report, known in Wales as "The Treason of the Blue Books", attacked Welsh as a language of slavery and ignorance, and condemned its use by pupils and teachers. Even among the Welsh themselves, use of the language was regarded as a social and economic obstacle, and determined efforts were made to stamp it out. This campaign culminated in the notorious **Welsh Not**, a system of punishment whereby children caught speaking Welsh were obliged to wear around the neck a wooden board, on which the words "Welsh Not" were painted. By 1901 the policy had taken its toll and only 50% of the population still spoke the Welsh language.

Demands for better educational provision had been growing during the 19C and in 1872 the first University College of Wales, funded by public donations, opened in a redundant hotel building in Aberystwyth.

Growth of National Feeling: 1920 to 1990s

As education became more accessible, new generations emerged of Welsh-speakers, schooled in English and staying in or returning to Wales to find professions. Members of this educated middle class were to play a leading part in the revival of national feeling and identity. Fears that Welsh culture would be lost altogether prompted a vigorous campaign to promote the use of Welsh in schools: one of the most energetic campaigners was **Owen M Edwards** (1858-1920), Chief Inspector of Schools in Wales, who published several Welsh-language magazines and books for children. He also founded Urdd Gobaith Cymru, the Welsh League of Youth which combined Christian and cultural ethics. In 1947 the first Welsh-language primary school was opened, to be followed in 1962 by the first bilingual secondary school, set up in the Anglicised industrial valleys of South Wales.

Political nationalism took on a more defined form after the First World War, and in 1925 the Welsh Nation-

© Wales Tourist Board

alist Party was founded by a group of writers and scholars which included the poet and author Saunders Lewis. In 1998 it changed its name to **Plaid Cymru** – the Party of Wales. Its appeal was largely to the agricultural, middle classes, and its emphasis lay on the Welsh language and culture. Industrial communities, disillusioned with Liberal government, turned to the growing Labour movement at a time of declining trade and increasing unemployment. **Aneurin Bevan** (1897-1960), an ex-miner who played a leading role in the miners' strike in 1926, was sent to parliament for Ebbw Vale in 1929; as Health Minister in the 1945 Labour government he introduced slum-clearance policies and laid the foundations of the National Health Service.

In the 1960s and 1970s nationalist feeling found a new voice in the **Welsh Language Society** *(Cymdeithas yr Iaith Gymraeg)*, whose followers staged demonstrations and defaced property in the name of the language. Piecemeal changes in the law brought more bilingualism into official life, adding Welsh to road signs, forms and court proceedings. In 1993 a Welsh Language Act stipulated that the Welsh language be treated, as far as is reasonably practicable, on the basis of equality with the English language in the public sector. It also set up the Welsh Language Board *(Bwrdd yr Iaith Gymraeg)*.

Administration and Economy: 1960s to 1990s

Welsh unemployment was running at twice the UK national average when the **Welsh Office** was established in 1964, giving Wales limited executive powers. This was followed by the creation of the **Welsh Development Agency (WDA)** in 1976, to encourage new economic initiatives. Under the reorganisation of local government in England and Wales in 1974, the 13 Welsh counties were replaced with eight new units, most taking the names of ancient principalities. Another reorganisation of local government in 1997 brought the return of many of the old county divisions.

In the latter part of the 20C there was growing support for a measure of devolution. The first referendum, held in 1979 – for a separate **Welsh Assembly**, without legislative powers – resulted in a majority against.

The 1980s brought radical changes to industrial Wales: by the middle of the decade every coal pit in the Rhondda Valley had been closed. Despite notable success in attracting foreign business to Welsh sites, former mining communities have continued to suffer from high unemployment and social dislocation.

The granting of a Welsh-language television channel – S4C – has encouraged a boom in the Welsh film, TV and animation industries.

Tourism is another area of economic success but there is widespread concern about its effects on rural society, and especially about the phenomenon of second homes and holiday cottages, which have changed the face of many communities, leaving some virtually deserted outside the tourist season.

In 1997 a second referendum on devolution produced a narrow majority (6 721 – 559 419 pro and 552 698 anti) in favour of the establishment of a **Welsh Assembly**. The parliamentary bill received the Royal Assent in the summer of 1998, making provision for elections to be held on 6 May 1999. The **Welsh Assembly** consists of 60 members, of which 40 are elected from the parliamentary constituencies and 20 from the five EU constituencies. There is simultaneous interpretation in Welsh and English and at present the members meet in Crickhowell House on Cardiff Bay. Discussions are in progress about the construction of a new building, to be designed by the winner of an architectural competition and erected in Cardiff, on a waterfront site looking outwards to the world.

Black Gold

In 1991 the post of President of the South Wales National Miners' Union was abolished, a sign that the long reign of King Coal in the South Wales mining valleys was effectively over. One of the heartlands of British industrial might, the South Wales coalfield stretched over a vast area between the eastern valleys and Pembrokeshire. At its zenith in the early years of the 20C nearly 60 million tons of coal were being extracted from the region's 600 or so pits, much of it of the superior "smokeless" quality which heated London homes and powered the locomotives of the Great Western Railway and the warships of the Royal Navy. The pithead winding gear rising from the valley bottom seemed an irreducible element of the Welsh landscape, as characteristic of the country as the close-knit mining communities themselves. By the 1920s, however, coal was in decline, ousted by oil on the oceans and affected by world-wide economic depression. The renowned radicalism of Welsh miners was seen in action for the last time in the bitter strike of 1984, when only a few dozen pits remained to be saved. By the mid-1990s, only one deep mine, Tower, was still in operation, though open-cast extraction, with all its attendant environmental problems, continued elsewhere.

Eisteddfod

No account of Welsh-language culture can ignore the **National Eisteddfod.** This festival-cum-contest-cum-fair is held every August, moving its sites from north to south Wales in alternate years. In a sense it acts as a substitute for permanent arts institutions, providing a stage for instrumentalists, singers, dancers, actors, writers and poets, and including a major exhibition of contemporary fine arts, sculpture and crafts.

■ Language

Perhaps the most apparent cultural division within Wales is that between Welsh-speakers and non-Welsh-speakers. During most of the 20C this corresponded to a great degree with the division between urban and rural Wales. Industrial communities in the south and south-east have tended to become Anglicised, while the farming and fishing communities of north and west Wales have remained predominantly Welsh-speaking. This situation has changed noticeably, though gradually, in the last few decades, as a revival of interest in the Welsh language has spread in the industrial towns, and as bilingual and Welsh-language institutions (such as the Welsh Development Agency, the Welsh Language Board and television and radio channels) have been established in the cities. Most official transactions can be carried out in Welsh and equality of treatment for the Welsh and English languages in the public sector was ensured by the Welsh Language Act 1993. Many place names have reverted to their original Welsh spelling but, where there is any chance of confusion, road signs are bilingual.

Three Cliffs Bay

■ Food and Drink

Although the Welsh food industry has played an important part in the British economy for centuries, the concept of Welsh cuisine has only very recently emerged. In the 1990s promoters have tried to make up for lost time, applying the **Taste of Wales** (*Blas ar Gymru*) accolade to home-grown products and to guesthouses, hotels and restaurants serving fresh local food in new or traditional recipes.

Seafood – The long Welsh coastline and its many rivers and lakes provide a wide range of freshwater and sea food, which is now enjoying a gradual revival after a post-war slump. Fish stalls sell fresh catches in Cardiff and Swansea central markets and in smaller ports around Cardigan Bay, and the famous Penclawdd cockles are still gathered on the Gower Peninsula and celebrated in Swansea's September Cockle Festival. Other seafood includes oysters, farmed at Pembroke and Anglesey; whiting, dogfish, crabs and lobsters, hauled in at Milford Haven, and King and Queen scallops from the Anglesey coast. Freshwater delicacies such as salmon and sewin (a pink-skinned sea trout) are fished from the rivers Wye, Teifi and Usk.

Laverbread, lettuce-like seaweed, is a unique Welsh seafood particularly popular in and around Swansea, where it is sold from the market stalls. It is usually served with bacon and can be bought fresh or in tins.

Meat – Lamb and beef have been a vital source of income in Wales since the Middle Ages. Until the 19C herds of sheep and cattle were regularly driven hundreds of miles from the Welsh mountains to English markets. The drovers who made these long and dangerous journeys became celebrated members of society and many of their routes can be followed and their resting places, the drovers' inns, visited.

Welsh lamb is now marketed all over the world as a lean and natural meat, while beef, traditionally overshadowed by the better-known lamb industry, has begun to profit from new promotion.

Dairy Products – A growing interest in old skills and recipes has brought new life to the Welsh dairy industry. **Caerphilly**, perhaps the most famous Welsh cheese, is creamy, white and mild; other cheeses include Llangloffan, which is red and flavoured with garlic, and Y Fenni, a type of cheddar with ale and mustard seed. Cheese-making is largely concentrated in Dyfed, where the shallow valleys and good pasture are ideal for dairy farms.

Welsh Dishes – Most traditional Welsh recipes were originally devised for maximum economy and nourishment rather than gastronomic excellence. *Cawl* is a thick broth of meat, vegetables and potatoes, still served as a standard winter meal. *Lobscaws* (pronounced Lobscouse), a stew made with left-overs, was the staple diet of poor Welsh communities in Liverpool in the 19C – hence the name "Scouse" for Liverpudlians. A mixture of hot milk and bread, sometimes thickened with an egg, *(bara-llaeth)* is unlikely to appear on many restaurant menus but a mash of swede and potatoes *(stwnsh rhwdans)* does occasionally make the transition from domestic to professional kitchen.

The **leek** is a popular ingredient in soups and sauces, or combined with potatoes or other vegetables. It is also worn as a national emblem.

Baking – Old baking recipes are still widely used and are familiar items on café menus. Perhaps the most popular is the Welsh cake, a cross between a biscuit and a currant scone, made like a drop-scone on an iron griddle and eaten, preferably warm, with butter or sugar, according to taste. Methods for baking *bara brith* (which means freckled bread), a rich fruit loaf, vary from cook to cook. Some recipes include spices, some treacle, and some require the fruit mixture to be soaked in tea overnight. A long "cut and come again" cake *(Teisen lap)*, which is less widely available, is made to a traditional Glamorgan recipe using currants and spices such as nutmeg.

Drinks – Beer is as popular in Wales as anywhere in Britain, despite (or perhaps because of) the Nonconformist temperance tradition. Beer-drinking is a long-established custom in British Legion clubs (set up for ex-servicemen) and sports clubs as well as pubs. Local brews include Brains Beer from Cardiff.

More recent ventures in the drinks industry have included a Welsh brand of whisky, Chwisgi, and Cariad wines, a range of award-winning whites and rosés grown in the Vale of Glamorgan. ■

SIGHTS

ABERAERON *

This trim little harbour town on the Cardigan coast owes its appeal to the ambitious improvements carried out at the beginning of the 19C by the local landowner. Before this time, Aberaeron had been little more than a fishing village huddled on higher ground a short distance inland away from the narrow coastal plain which suffered frequent flooding and changes of course by the capricious River Aeron.

The Reverend Alban Thomas Jones Gwynne may well have had the advice of John Nash in constructing the stone piers and quays and the two squares around which the new, harmoniously **planned port town** was laid out. Building began in 1807 and proceeded throughout the first half of the 19C, leaving a legacy of fine **terraced houses** whose sobriety of design is set off by well-considered detailing of windows, doors and cornerstones as well as by cheerful colour schemes. The exotic names of some of the houses recall the vessels sailed in by their owners.

Aberaeron's harbour flourished until the early 20C, with a lively coastal trade and considerable shipbuilding activity, mostly of smacks and schooners. The railways eventually killed the coastal trade, though Aberaeron was linked to the national rail network only in 1911. The last steamship set out in 1934 and the last steam train ran in 1963 but the town continues to thrive as a holiday place, the harbour full of pleasure boats and the quaysides of strolling visitors. ■

Ceredigion – Population 1 493
Michelin Atlas p 24 or Map 503
H 27
Tourist Information Centre
– The Quay, Aberaeron
SA46 0BT ☎ 01545 570 602;
Fax 01970 626 566; aberaeronT
IC@ceredigion.gov.uk

Beaches – At Aberaeron South, New Quay and Cwmtudu.
Craft Centre – Craftsmen and women can be seen at work in the 18 workshops of the **Aberaeron Craft Centre** (*behind Holy Trinity Church on A 487*).

ABERGAVENNY*

This bustling market town on a glacial mound just above the Usk is overlooked by a number of hills, of which the most distinctive are Sugar Loaf, Blorenge and Skirrid. Once a Roman garrison, then a Norman borough, Abergavenny prospered as early industrial development started in the Clydach Gorge and on the southern fringes of the Brecon Beacons.

The castle is in ruins and the town's defensive walls and gateways have long since disappeared but, although the townscape is a mixture of Georgian, Victorian and modern, older edifices lurk behind many a more recent façade.

A walk around the town centre reveals a number of fine buildings, among them old inns like the black-and-white **Angel** in Cross Street, arcaded and jettied-out shops in **Market Street**, and the old **Cow Inn** in Nevill Street, once the town residence of the owners

(Y-Fenni) Monmouthshire – Population 9 593 Michelin Atlas p 16 or Map 503 L 28 Tourist Information Centre – Swan Meadow, Monmouth Road, Abergavenny NP7 5HH ☎ 01873 857 588; Fax 01873 850 217; abergavenny-tic@tsww.com

of Tretower Court, and splendidly decorated with dragons and the heads of goats as well as cows. The dominant structure is the copper-clad tower of the **Town Hall** of 1870.

Monuments★★ – The collection of effigies is one of the finest and most extensive in Great Britain, many of the local lords having chosen to be buried in the priory church. After years of neglect, these superb figures are now being restored. ■

ABERYSTWYTH★★

Gazing resolutely seaward, the gently curving Victorian terraces of this "Welsh Brighton" make it one of the most distinctive of the Welsh seaside resorts, held firmly in the centre of the great arc of Cardigan Bay by the heights to north and south. Aberystwyth's history goes back much further than the arrival of the first tourists towards the end of the 18C. The southern height, Pendinas, is crowned by an Iron Age hillfort of about 600 BC, while the headland near the twin estuary of the Rheidol and Ystwyth carries the remains of a late-13C castle, one of the chain of strongholds built by Edward I to keep the Welsh in check. At first only Englishmen were permitted to settle in the walled town protected by the castle, but the Welsh soon found ways of circumventing this restriction and the population has long been a mixed one.

Aberystwyth's first wave of popularity came at the end of the 18C, when war with the French made foreign travel risky. A second wave followed the building of the railway in 1864. Since the late 19C, with the foundation of the first University College of Wales (1872) and the establishment of the National Library

Ceredigion – Population 8 359
Michelin Atlas p 24 or Map 503
H 26
Tourist Information Centre
– Terrace Road, Aberystwyth
SY23 2AG ☎ 01970 612 125;
Fax 01970 626 566; aberystwyth
TIC@ceredigion.gov.uk

(1907), Aberystwyth has become a stronghold of Welshness.

The Seafront (Marine Terrace)★ (AX) – Recently partly repaved and dipping slightly towards the gravelly beach, the broad promenade is backed by an undulating line of three- and four-storey pastel-coloured 19C hotels and boarding houses, their myriad windows reflecting the rays of the sun as it sets over the bay. No recent intrusions mar the extraordinary homogeneity of this Victorian seaside townscape. The **Pier**, reputed to be 800ft/243m long at the time of its building in 1865, has been gnawed at by the sea over the years and is now sadly truncated. The fulcrum of the seafront is formed by the bandstand, while its northern limit is marked by the somewhat grim stone façades of Alexandra Hall, once a female students' hostel.

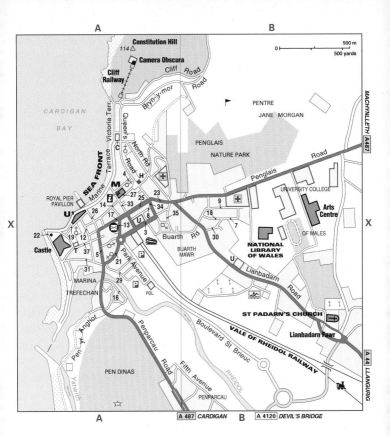

Out and About
Arts Centre – The centre *(see below)* provides a continuous pro-gramme of exhibitions, theatre and other performances.
Beaches – At Aberystwyth North and South; at Clarach Bay and Borth *(N)* and at Llanrhystud **(S)**.

The rugged slopes of **Constitu-tion Hill (AX)** are no longer gar-dened as intensively as they were a century ago, and the amusements of Luna Park which occupied the summit (430ft/132m) have long since been dismantled, but the **Cliff Railway (AX)** of 1896 still travels up and down its vertigi-nous track (778ft/237m long) and the **Camera Obscura** removed in the 1920s has been replaced by a worthy successor incorporating half a ton of sophisticated optics which give an extraordinary pano-rama of the town in its spectacular setting of ocean and mountain.

Aberystwyth Castle (AX) – The first castle, a largely timber struc-ture, had been built in 1110 on the banks of the Ystwyth. Edward I's replacement, one of the first as well as one of the largest of his Welsh strongholds, began to rise from the promontory near the mouth of the Rheidol in 1277 consisting of two concentric dia-monds of walls and towers and with a massive inner gatehouse-cum-keep. It was taken by Owain Glyn Dŵr in 1404, housed French prisoners captured at Agincourt, and was besieged in the Civil War,

after which it was blown up; the remaining fragments do indeed lie around the grassy headland as if scattered by a mighty explosion. The most substantial remains are those of a wall tower and of the Great Gatehouse facing the town.

Town Centre – The approximate line of the walls enclosing the English bastide town on its low rise can be traced in the align-ment of King Street, Alfred Place, Baker Street, Chalybeate Street, Mill Street and South Road.

One of the more striking buildings from the heyday of Aberystwyth is the ebullient stone and terracotta Coliseum Theatre of 1904, now the **Ceredigion Museum (AX M)**.

National Library of Wales (BX)★– This solemn, municipal-looking building in pale stone stands high above the town just below the campus of the Univer-sity College at Penglais. It is one of the United Kingdom's legal deposit libraries, holding more than 3.5 million printed works, 40 000 manuscripts, 4 million deeds and documents as well as works of art, photographs and audio-visual material. ∎

BRECON*

Brecon's strategic location, midway on the Roman road west from Gloucester to Carmarthen, was appreciated by the Normans, who built a castle overlooking the confluence of the Usk with the Honddu in 1093. The borough which grew up under the protection of Bernard de Neufmarche's stronghold was defended by 10 towers and four gateways, long since demolished, but the intricate and fascinating street layout of medieval Brecon remains intact. Many of its older houses were rebuilt or given fashionable Georgian façades in the 18C and 19C as the town consolidated its position as the focal point of much of southern mid-Wales.

Brecon remains an important agricultural centre and has a significant military presence too. For much of the year its streets are trodden by tourists, pausing here on the way west – the Romans' route has become the modern highway (A 40) – or using the town as their base for exploration of the Brecon Beacons National Park, whose

(Aberhonddu) Powys – Population 7 523
Michelin Atlas pp 16 and 25 or Map 503 J 28
Tourist Information Centre – Cattle Market Car Park, Brecon LD3 9DA ☏ 01874 622 485; Fax 01874 625 256.

highest point, Pen-y-Fan, rises half concealed among lesser summits a short distance to the south.

Brecon Cathedral* – The "most splendid and dignified church in mid-Wales" (Richard Haslam), once the centrepiece of a Benedictine priory, became the town's parish church at the Dissolution and was elevated to cathedral status in 1923. It stands in well-tree'd surroundings above the Honddu at a discreet distance from the town centre and retains a number of its conventual buildings, one of which, a 16C tithe barn, has been converted into an attractive **heritage centre**, housing an exhibition which traces the history of the priory and the life of the medieval monks. ∎

Out and About

Craft Centre – Beacons Crafts *(Bethel Square)* is a cooperative shop formed by local craft producers displaying the selected work of 50 makers.

BRECON BEACONS★★

Carmarthenshire, Powys, Rhondda Cynon Taff, Merthyr Tydfil, Monmouthshire

The Brecon Beacons stretch from from east to west, a glorious tract of rolling mountain country (40mi/65km) between the crowded industrial valleys of the south and the empty uplands of mid-Wales.

The area, which was designated a **National Park** in 1957, consists of four main blocks, all with the same geological foundation of Old Red Sandstone. The core is formed by the **Brecon Beacons** themselves, which include the highest peaks in South Wales, Corn Du (2 863ft/873m) and Pen-y-Fan (2 906ft/886m), looking northward to the fertile valley of the Usk. To the west is **Fforest Fawr**, a vast rolling upland giving way in the south to fascinating limestone country around Ystradfellte, with its crags and caves, wooded ravines and waterfalls. The **Black Mountain** forms the westernmost block, its lonely centrepiece the remote crags of the Carmarthen Vans (2 460ft/750m). The eastern heights, confusingly named the **Black Mountains**, consist of a spectacular escarpment overlooking the valley of the Wye, behind which long, winding valleys drain southwards towards Abergavenny and the Usk.

Michelin Atlas pp 15 and 16 or Map 503 J 28
Tourist Information Centre – Beaufort Chambers, Beaufort Street, Crickhowell NP8 1AA
☎ *01873 812 105.*

The proximity of the Brecon Beacons to large centres of population has made the National Park a favourite destination with day visitors, who outnumber tourists by about two to one. The more popular and accessible places are often crowded, but it is easy to find other spots where relative solitude can be enjoyed.

■ **Eastern section** – *East of the road (A 470) between Brecon and Merthyr Tydfil*

Pen-y-Fan★★ – The dramatic north-facing escarpment of the Brecon Beacons is revealed in all its majesty to those who have made the climb to the top of South Wales' highest mountain. The precipitous upper slopes, the deep embayments or cwms, and the U-shaped valleys are the work of glaciers, one of which also

Out and About

Information Centres – The best starting point for exploring the Brecon Beacons National Park is the **Brecon Beacons Mountain Centre** *(see below)*, which provides a wide range of information and other facilities. The **Craig-y-Nos Country Park** *(see below)* offers lakes, riverside walks, mature woodland and meadows. Short residential courses providing detailed study and exploration of the Beacons are organised by the **Danywenallt Study Centre**.

Beacons Bus – The Beacons Bus service, which enables visitors to leave their cars behind and thus avoid congestion in the park, operates in summer on Sundays and bank holidays, between Brecon and other points both within the park and beyond its boundaries.

Weather Conditions – Mountain walkers should bear in mind that temperatures drop rapidly as height is gained, roughly by 2 C for every 1 000ft/300m. This, combined with wind-chill, can mean that summit conditions can be unpleasantly, even dangerously, different from those which seemed so encouraging at the starting point of a climb down in the valley. All the usual precautions should be taken before setting out.

Walking – This is the dominant recreational activity. Good walking is provided by the foothills and ridges of the **Black Mountains** (south of Hay-on-Wye), the **Taff Trail** (between Brecon and Merthyr Tydfil), the **Usk Valley Walk** along the towpath of the Monmouthshire and Brecon Canal and the Clydach Gorge (including Gilwern). The ascent of **Pen-Y-Fan** from near *Storey Arms* on the main road (A 470) is both popular and relatively easy (climb of only some 1 650ft/500m). Longer but less frequented routes to the summit start from the Neuadd reservoir to the SE (climb of c 3 000ft/900m) or from small parking areas at the head of narrow lanes to the north.

Pony-trekking – There are many centres which organise **pony-trekking** for whole or half days.

Caving – There are opportunities for caving in the extensive limestone systems in the south-west area of the Park.

Brecon Mountain Railway – *At Dowlais, 2.5mi/4km north of Merthyr Tydfil.* The old Brecon and Merthyr Railway across the mountains of the Brecon Beacons was one of the highest, most spectacular, and least profitable in Britain. In the severe winter of 1947, a train was stuck in snow near the summit of the line for several days. All services ceased in 1964, but since 1980 a narrow-gauge line has been steadily colonising the old trackbed north from a new station at Pant, and visitors can now enjoy a round trip *(7mi/11km)* into the uplands.

Monmouthshire and Brecon Canal – There are **narrowboats** for hire at Brecon, at Storehouse Bridge between Llanfrynach and Pencelli, Talybont, Llangynidr and Gilwern *(see also below)*.

Fishing – The Wye, Usk and Tywi are famous for their **salmon fishing**. Many reservoirs are stocked with **trout** and there is **coarse fishing** in Llangorse Lake and in the Monmouthshire and Brecon Canal.

Water Sports – There is **boating, canoeing** and **sailing** on Llangorse Lake, the River Usk and the River Wye.

created the perfect shape of **Llyn Cwm Llwch**, the lake at the foot of Pen-y-Fan. The structure and colour of the underlying Old Red Sandstone, formed in desert conditions in Devonian times some 395-345 million years ago, gives a delicately ribbed pattern to the steep escarpment. A particularly resistant combination of sandstone and conglomerate caps the summit of both Pen-y-Fan and its near neighbour, Corn Du, creating the effect of paving. Bronze Age people built burial cairns, recently excavated and restored, on both peaks.

Llangorse Lake – This is the largest natural lake (over 1mi/1.5km long) in South Wales, fringed with reedbeds, alders and willows, and an important habitat for wetland birds. It also attracts campers and caravanners and all kinds of water activities not always compatible with its wildlife. The lake is the site of a fascinating artificial island (crannog), constructed around the 9C AD from layers of stone, earth and brushwood held in place by oaken palisades.

Castell Dinas – The very fragmentary ruins of this 12C stronghold, which was the highest castle in Great Britain (alt 1 476ft/450m), are contained within the more impressive remains of an Iron-Age **hillfort** with multiple ramparts. The car park is a starting point for a steep walk on the pathways leading to the boggy summit of the Black Mountains, Waun Fach (2 660ft/811m), or, more interestingly, along the spectacular escarpment which looks towards the hills of Radnorshire across the exhilaratingly broad valley of the Wye.

Penyclawdd Court* – *5mi/8km N of Abergavenny near Llanfihangel Crucorney; from A 465 turn left opposite sign to Pantygelli onto minor road and follow signs for Penyclawdd Farm.* This beautifully restored Tudor manor house was built in 1480, extended in the early

Park Pen-y-fan

17C and passed through several families, including the Cecils and the Herberts (the family of the poet George Herbert). Interesting features include a rare 17C door lintel (most were removed as the average height increased) and a pre-spring bed, made with frame and tautened rope (hence the expression "sleep tight"). A Norman motte with wet and dry moats rises in the grounds; recent herb and knot gardens and a maze have been planted and a terraced garden in Tudor style is planned.

Crickhowell – *6mi/10km W of Abergavenny by A 40*. Despite its small size, Crickhowell has a confident air of urbanity about it; in 1804 Richard Fenton called it "the most cheerful-looking town I ever saw". The townscape has changed little since, and Crickhowell is popular both with residents and with tourists using it as a base from which to explore the Brecon Beacons National Park. The name of the town derives from Crug Hywel, the stronghold of **Hywel Dda** *(see index)*, which was built on Table Mountain, dominating the town.

There are two focal points, **Crickhowell Bridge**, one of the finest of several bridges along the Usk, and the **Square**, with a fountain and *The Bear,* a Georgian coaching inn. The bridge was in place in the 15C but was rebuilt in 1706 with cutwaters and, oddly, 12 arches on one side and 13 on the other. Between bridge and square runs the High Street, with good 18C-19C buildings including *The Dragon* with its Venetian window, and then Bridge Street, twisting and falling to the *Bridge End Inn,* once an octagonal toll-house.

Clydach Gorge – *3.5mi/6km W of Abergavenny by A 465 (Heads of the Valleys Road) and then along minor roads (signs)*. This deep, narrow valley provides a vivid picture of the course of industrial history over some 200 years. Iron-making was a going concern here in the 17C and grew rapidly, as technology advanced and demand increased, but declined in the 19C, unable to overcome the difficulties of this steep terrain; limestone however continued to be quarried. Various trails have been marked out from the Clydach Gorge picnic area, taking in some of the industrial remains, including the Clydach ironworks and lime works, the 19C Llammarch tramroad and the 18C aqueduct of the Brecknock and Abergavenny Canal *(Some steep ascents and descents; visitors should keep to the public footpaths as some areas are potentially dangerous)*.

Monmouthshire and Brecon Canal – The Monmouthshire and Brecon Canal (33mi/53km long), the only British canal entirely within a National Park, runs southeast from its terminal in Brecon to just south of

Pontypool. It was completed in 1812 and connected the interior with the coast at Newport and served local collieries, ironworks and limestone quarries, as well as carrying agricultural produce and passengers. Like most such enterprises, its period of prosperity was short. From the mid-19C onwards, its trade went to the railways, and the last commercial toll was collected in 1933.

A new lease of life began in the 1960s when the canal's exceptional recreational potential was realised. A contour canal, winding its way along the lower slopes of the enchanting valley of the Usk and flanking the dramatic scenery of the Brecon Beacons, it has only six locks in its entire length and one section of 22mi/35km is entirely lock-free. Engineering features include lift bridges, the Talybont tunnel and the fine Brynich aqueduct over the Usk.

■ **Western section** – *West of the road (A 470) between Brecon and Merthyr Tydfil*

Brecon Beacons Mountain Centre – *5mi/8 km SW of Brecon by A 470.* This National Park visitor centre, opened in 1966, was the first of its kind in Great Britain, and proved immensely popular from the moment of its inception. The centre stands at a height of 1 100ft/335m on **Mynydd Illtud**, a splendid upland tract with enticing views immediately to the south of the escarpments of Fforest Fawr and the Brecon Beacons themselves. The centre offers a wide range of information – walks on Mynydd Illtud Common – and other facilities.

Garwnant Forestry Commission Visitor Centre – *6mi/9.5km N of Merthyr Tydfil by A 470 and a long winding side road (brown signs).* The Visitor Centre, which occupies a picturesque setting next to the Llwyn Onn Reservoir, interprets the natural world of the forests of the Brecon Beacons; there are woodland walks to suit all capacities and cycles routes marked out in the surrounding woodland, as well as special trails for the disabled. The centre offers wayfaring and orienteering courses.

Ystradfellte ★ – *W of Merthyr Tydfil by A 465 and N by minor road. Car parks may be crowded; the pathways have been severely eroded and are potentially dangerous in places, although improvements are under way. Check locally about access to the waterfalls. The caves can be a trap for the unwary and should not be entered.*

The River Mellte flows over a series of fine **waterfalls** downstream from this tiny hamlet in the southern part of Fforest Fawr, first carving itself a miniature, delightfully wooded gorge before disappearing into the gaping maw of **Porth yr Ogof** (50ft/15m wide). This cave, a favourite with potholers, is one of the most extraordinary features of the Carboniferous Limestone country of this part of the Park, swallowing the river until, equally surprisingly, it re-emerges a short distance downstream.

The limit of the soft and permeable limestone and the presence of the harder rocks of the Millstone Grit is marked by the first of the Mellte waterfalls, **Sgwd Clungwyn** (White Meadow Fall) about 0.75mi/1km downstream from the river's resurgence. Then come **Sgwd Clun-gwyn Isaf** (Lower White Meadow Fall) and **Sgwd y Pannwr** (Fuller's Fall), while on the Hepste, a tributary of the Mellte, there is **Sgwd yr Eira** (Fall of Snow), where it is possible to walk behind the curtain of water.

Dan-yr-Ogof Showcaves★ – *On A 4067.* The action of water on the Carboniferous Limestone overlying the Old Red Sandstone along the southern margin of the National Park has created some of the most fascinating cave formations open to the public in Britain.

In the upper valley of the River Tawe, the caves were discovered only in 1912, when the Morgan brothers from Abercrave boldly made their way underground, ferrying themselves across a small lake by coracle and reaching a powerful waterfall. Further exploration was carried out in the 1930s and 1960s, and today some of the more spectacular sections of this world beneath the surface has been made accessible, with ingenious lighting effects, tableaux and recorded commentaries.

Black Mountain★ – *E of Llandeilo on A 4069. Lake and ridge are accessible only on foot, from the village of Llanddeusant.* Something of the bleak character of this westernmost section of the National Park can be appreciated from the main road (A 4069) between Llangadog and Brynamman which climbs to a height of nearly 1 640ft/500m at Foel Fawr. To the northeast are the slopes leading up to **Carmarthen Fans** *(Bannau Sir Gâr),* a great pointed ridge with near-vertical walls dropping to two lakes, Llyn y Fan Fawr and **Llyn y Fan Fach**. According to legend, a fairy maiden rising from the waters of the latter helped found a dynasty of healers which lasted from the 13C until the 19C, though she returned to the lake when her husband inadvertently broke her spell. ■

CAERLEON ROMAN FORTRESS★★

Newport

Together with the other legionary fortresses at Chester (Deva) and Wroxeter (Viroconium), Caerleon (Isca) controlled the entire system of forts and highways by which the tribes of Wales were held in subjection. Substantial remains of amphitheatre, baths, barracks, and fortress walls testify to the imprint left on Wales by the centuries of Roman occupation, and, even though partly obscured by the later development of the little town of Caerleon, this is one of the most important and evocative Roman sites in Britain.

Fortress Baths★ – The shell of this extraordinary complex of baths and leisure facilities survived into the Middle Ages. Some of it now lies beneath later buildings, but the long and narrow **swimming pool** (natatio) and part of the **changing room** (apodyterium) and **cold room** (frigidarium) are well displayed beneath the viewing galleries of the splendid new cover building.

Legionary Museum★ – The well-presented collection of sculpture, mosaics, pottery, glass and other artefacts evokes life as lived in the

Michelin Atlas p 16 or Map 503 L 29
Tourist Information Centre – 5 High Street, Caerleon NP6 1AE
@/Fax 01633 422 656.

legionary fortress. The most-prized exhibits are the **88** engraved **gemstones** found when the drain of the baths was being excavated. The collection was begun in 1850 as a reaction to the unsupervised plundering of the site of Caerleon which had gone on since the late 18C, and the modern building retains the Classical portico of the edifice erected at that time.

Amphitheatre★ – The Legion's amphitheatre was built just outside the fortress walls c AD 90, making it contemporary with the Colosseum in Rome. Fully excavated in the 1920s, it is perhaps the finest of its kind in Britain and, although the sand of the arena has been replaced by grass, can still evoke the days when it could provide the entire garrison of 5 000 with the often gruesome spectacles to which they were accustomed. Oval in shape, it consists of massive earth banks reinforced in stone. ■

CAERPHILLY CASTLE★★

(Caerffili) Caerphilly

This spectacular late-13C castle, standing implacably in its valley setting of great defensive lakes, ranks among the most formidable strongholds of the realm. Its innovative concentric design served as a model for Edward I's castles in North Wales, but the King's triumph in the north in 1282 removed the threat Caerphilly had been intended to counter. It remains as potent a statement of military power as any in British history.

Michelin Atlas p 16 or Map 503 K 29
Tourist Information Centre – The Twyn, Caerphilly CF83 1JL
☎ *029 2088 0011; Fax 029 2086 0811; tourismpaul@compuserve.com*

■ Historical notes

The Romans built a stronghold here, on the road connecting their major forts at Cardiff and Y Gaer near Brecon. Nearly 1 200 years later, in 1268 **Gilbert de Clare** began work on his castle, which was swiftly completed in spite of its vast extent; Caerphilly was intended to deter **Llywelyn the Last** (ap Gruffydd), the last native Prince of Wales, from any thought of interfering with Norman hegemony in this part of the country. Well aware of the threat it represented, Llywelyn seized the fortress in 1270 when it was only half-finished. De Clare regained control by a trick and work pro-

ceeded apace, the castle being substantially complete a year later. Llywelyn retired north into the uplands in grim acceptance of this limit set to his ambitions. His defeat and death and the consequent subjugation of the whole country to English control meant that Caerphilly was no longer needed as a frontier fortress, though it continued as the administrative centre for the De Clare estates. It was attacked by Welsh rebels in 1295 but, although the town was burnt down, the castle held out.

In the early 14C the castle's owner was Edward II's favourite, **Hugh le Despenser**, and the King himself sheltered here in the course of the campaign conducted against him by his Queen Isabella and her lover Mortimer. Later generations found the giant stronghold lacking in domestic amenity and preferred more comfortable residences elsewhere. Caerphilly decayed, its stone being plundered for the building of a nearby country house, The Van, and its walls being undermined as the unmaintained lakes dried out. In the Civil War an earthwork was built to the northwest and some deliberate demolition of the castle's defences may have taken place.

The borough of Caerphilly prospered during the Age of Coal, and it was coal money that came to the derelict castle's rescue. As well as pouring their millions into the re-creation of their castles at Cardiff and Castell Coch, the **Bute** family took Caerphilly in hand, protecting the ruins from further damage, removing the houses that had been built up against the walls and carrying out a meticulous programme of restoration. After the castle had passed into state ownership in 1950, the lakes were once more filled with water.

■ Tour

Outer works – *Limited parking by the Tourist Information Centre close to the Main Outer Gate; more extensive parking west of the castle (10min walk).*

On a bend in the Rhymney River, Caerphilly is separated from Cardiff and the Glamorgan coast by the abrupt upland of Caerphilly Common. With the removal of the buildings impudently erected against its walls and with water in its lakes once more, the castle has emerged from its entanglement with its once-dependent town and can be seen in all its magnificence. The walk from the western car park enables the sheer extent of the defences to be appreciated. De Clare had been impressed by the artificial lakes at Kenilworth Castle, where he had helped in the siege of Simon de Montfort's forces in 1266. At Caerphilly he ordered some of the most elaborate water engineering of medieval times to be carried out, involving the damming of the marshy valleys of two streams to form two great lakes as well as inner and outer moats. A **hornwork**, an artificial island now known as the West Platform, was created to lend strength to the defences on the west. Beyond this to the north is the site of the **Roman fort** on which the **Civil War earthwork** was raised. No less spectacular than the lakes are the **dams** themselves; the earth platform of the southern dam is reinforced in stone, defended by a tower and a gateway, and has a line of massive buttresses on its outer face. The northern dam also has a gateway, although subsidence has caused the projecting towers to break away from the wall.

Outer and Inner Wards – The castle is approached across its outer moat via the formidable **Main Outer Gate** with its array of defensive features. It served for many years as a prison and now contains extensive displays on the castle's history.

Beyond the inner moat looping round from the south lake is the core of the castle, the concentric prototype for the royal strongholds in the north like Beaumaris. The curtain wall of the outer ward is entered via a relatively modest gatehouse, beyond which is the massive **East Inner Gatehouse** defending the Inner Ward, designed to resist an attacker who might have gained control of the rest of the castle. Its apartments were probably occupied by the castle's constable. Of the corner towers, the **Southeast Tower** is the least modified, with original arrowslits and battlements; it leans at an alarming angle, probably the result of subsidence. The splendid **Northwest Tower** houses further displays, but the finest structure in the Inner Ward is the **Great Hall,** remodelled by Hugh le Despenser to provide a sumptuous setting for lordly life. Reroofed by the Butes in the 19C, it has magnificent windows in the Decorated style, while one of the corbels seems to have been carved in the likeness of Edward II. ■

CARDIFF★★★

Cosmopolitan Cardiff is the Principality's administrative, business and cultural capital as well as the focal point of a vast urban region encompassing much of South Wales. Hardly more than a village at the start of the 19C, and thus accustomed to rapid change, the city looks forward to an increasingly dynamic role in a Europe committed to revitalisation of its regions. Its role as the capital of the Principality has been reinforced by the presence of the Welsh Assembly, elected in 1999 and due to occupy its own waterfront building some time in the third millennium.

(Caerdydd) Cardiff – Population 279 055
Michelin Atlas p 16 or Map 503 K 29
Cardiff Tourist Information Centre – 16 Wood Street, Cardiff CF10 1ES
☎ *029 2022 7281; Fax 029 2023 9162.*

■ Historical notes

Cardiff grew up under the protection of the Norman castle built on the site of the Roman fort commanding the crossing of the tidal River Taff. It remained just one among Wales' many small harbour towns and trading centres until the end of the 18C, when the ironmasters and colliery owners of the Valleys sought an outlet to the sea for their burgeoning enterprises. The Glamorganshire Canal opened in 1798 to Merthyr Tydfil, the Taff Vale Railway to Merthyr and the Rhondda in the 1840s. By the start of the 20C Cardiff was one of the world's great ports, exporting 10.5 million tons of coal annually, and its population had swelled from a mere thousand or two to 182 000.

This phenomenal growth was due in large part to the vision of the second **Marquess of Bute** (1793-1848) of Cardiff Castle, who invested his fortune in the construction of Bute West Dock, the beginning of the city's modern harbour. The vast wealth this "creator of modern Cardiff" passed on to the Third Marquess (1847-1900) was partly ploughed back into further harbour developments, partly spent on the extraordinary metamorphosis of Cardiff Castle into a dream palace of the Middle Ages. In the 20C the decline of coal and iron has been offset by the city's forceful adoption of other roles, in government and culture

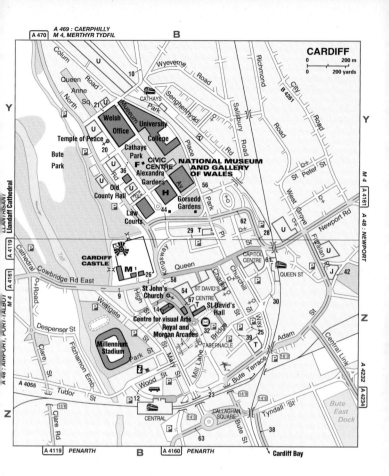

Out and About

Sightseeing – A good way to see the major sights is to board one of the open-top buses for the **Guide Friday Cardiff Bus Tour**, which circles the city centre, and drop off or reboard at any of the stopping places - Castle Museum, National Museum, Queen Street Station, Pier Head (Maritime Museum), Stuart Street (Techniquest), Mill Lane (shopping), Central Bus Station (TIC).

Cardiff Card combines free public transport with free entry to all top attractions in and around Cardiff and discounts on selected restaurants, cafés, craft and gift shops, entertainment venues, car hire and coach tours.

Shopping – **Craft in the Bay** – *(Bute Street)* Shopwindow for the work of members of the Makers Guild of Wales – ceramics, glass, textiles, jewellery, wood and basketware. ☏ 01222 756 428.

Entertainment – Cardiff has a lively cultural scene, including the Welsh Proms, Welsh National Opera, the Cardiff Singer of the World competition (June), a Festival of Folk Dancing (June) and a Summer Festival (July and August) comprising comedy, street entertainment, children's events, free open-air concerts and fairground fun.

St David's Hall is a concert hall (1 900 seats) with bars and restaurants; home of the BBC National Orchestra of Wales (NOW). The Hayes. ☏ 01222 878 444 (Box Office).

New Theatre *(Park Place)*, an Edwardian theatre (900 seats), recently restored, puts on performances (three seasons per annum) by the Welsh National Opera Company, and other theatrical productions. ☏ 01222 878 889.

Cardiff International Arena *(Mary Ann Street)* is a concert and exhibition venue with bar and restaurant. ☏ 01222 224 488.

The **Sherman Theatre** *(Senghenydd Road)* consists of two modern theatres with programme of drama and cinema with bar and café. ☏ 01222 230 451, 396 844.

The **Chapter Arts Centre** *(Market Road)* comprises cinemas, theatres, exhibition and workshop spaces, studio and café, presenting contemporary arts, music and culture. ☏ 01222 230 451.

The **Wales Millennium Centre**, funded by a grant from the Millennium Commission and erected on a waterfront site, will be a new arts centre, providing a home for Welsh National Opera and a stage for West End musicals from London; it will also house a cinema with a giant screen.

The **Atlantic Wharf Leisure Village** *(Hemingway Road)* is a themed leisure complex with a multi-screen cinema, bowling arena, restaurants and shops. ☏ 01222 471444.

Sport – **Millennium Stadium**, erected on the site of the former **Cardiff Arms Park** stadium, is the new home of the national game – Rugby football.

– best expressed in the gleaming white palaces of its spacious Civic Centre – and in commerce, visible everyday in the teeming life of city centre streets and arcades. Cardiff's focus shifted northwards away from the port, and busy Butetown lost its dynamism, leaving the great structures of the 19C boom like the Coal Exchange and the Pierhead Building without a fitting function. By the 1980s the tide had turned; a Development Corporation is now overseeing the reintegration of the historic waterfront and city centre with an array of ambitious proposals. The catalyst for these is a barrage across the entrance to Cardiff Bay, which will still the great tides (40ft/12m) of the Bristol Channel and hide the mudflats for ever beneath a freshwater lake (500 acres/200ha), a fit setting for such prestige projects as Welsh National Opera and a purpose-built home for the National Assembly for Wales.

■ City centre

Cardiff's principal axis, lined with a variegated mixture of 19C and early-20C shops and other buildings, is formed by St Mary Street and High Street. Aligned on the Castle gateway, this was the principal thoroughfare of the medieval town, with long burgage plots of land running away at right angles. This ancient pattern is still apparent in the **arcades (BZ)** extending eastwards, which are one of the most attractive features of the city centre; like the bustling **covered market,** these date from the confident days of Victorian commercialism and are lined with specialist shops of all kinds. Both Royal and Morgan Arcades still have original 19C shopfronts.

Arcades and lanes lead to busy pedestrianised areas centred on Hayes Island, where buses and taxis pick up their passengers by the statue of the city's 19C radical reformer John Batchelor.

Contrasting civic styles are seen in the resolutely modern **St David's Hall (BZ)**, modelled on the New Philharmonia in Berlin, and the **Centre for Visual Arts (BZ)**, which was built in 1882 and has been converted into a multi-purpose arts centre.

To the north is the parish **Church of St John (BZ),** whose elegant Perpendicular tower (130ft/40m) remains a city centre landmark. Inside, the Lady Chapel has an unusual Jacobean monument to two brothers, Sir William Herbert and Sir John Herbert, the latter Chief Secretary to Queen Elizabeth and King James I as well as Ambassador to Denmark, Poland, and to "Henri IV, King of the Gauls". A tiny carving of a non-spherical leather ball, a modest reminder of the Welsh passion for Rugby football, can be seen in the Priory Chapel.

To the east, several city blocks have been redeveloped as the **St David's Centre**, the contemporary equivalent of the 19C arcades. Several of the exits from the Centre connect it with Queen Street, which has also been much redeveloped, although Queen's Chambers, a wonderful Venetian palazzo (c 1877), still stands by the site of the old East Gate.

Between the city centre and the east bank of the River Taff rise four white cantilevered towers suppporting the roof of the gigantic **Millennium Stadium**, an unavoidable reminder of the place of Rugby football in the life of the Welsh nation, which replaces the former stadium in **Cardiff Arms Park (BZ)**, originally a piece of marshy land given by the Marquess of Bute for cricket and other games. The first international rugby game (with Ireland) took place here in 1884. To see the excellent facilities and look down from the top tier of seating, take the guided tour – dressing rooms, press box, TV studio and hospitality boxes; better still go to a match to listen to the Welsh crowd singing and to hear the roar when a goal is scored. If you are not a rugby fan book a seat for one of the many sporting and musical events which take place in the arena; the turf is removed between matches.

■ Cardiff castle** (BZ)

Deflecting city centre traffic to east and west, the Castle's high curtain wall closes the vista up the High Street and proclaims the long-standing importance of this site, which, fortified by Romans and Normans, became in the 19C a supreme expression of Victorian wealth, confidence and imagination. The Romans' fort guarded the point where their military road crossed the Taff on its way from

© Wales Tourist Board

the legionary station at Caerleon to Carmarthen. Part of the Roman wall (10ft/3m thick) is visible today, distinguished from later construction by a band of red stone; an impressive section can be inspected at close quarters below ground inside the castle.

The Normans' first castle – a timber structure atop a motte – was stormed by a local Welsh ruler in 1158, and was replaced at the end of the 12C by the superb 12-sided **shell keep** which still dominates the precinct today. In the 13C, **Gilbert de Clare** strengthened the defences further, giving the keep a new gatehouse and building the Black Tower. In the more peaceful conditions of the 15C, living accommodation, including a hall and the Octagon Tower, was built along the west wall of the castle.

In the late 18C the castle became the property of the Bute family, and the process began of converting the castle into a luxurious home. The First Marquess brought in Capability Brown and Henry Holland to "landscape the Grounds and modernise the Lodgings" but it was the Third Marquess and his architect **William Burges** (1827-81), with their shared passion for an idealised Middle Ages, who were responsible for the present fantastic appearance of much of the castle.

Work began in 1867 with the demolition of a row of houses built against the south wall, and continued with construction of the **Clock Tower** at the wall's southwest angle. The external appearance of the tower with its complex skyline, painted statues and heraldic shields gives a bare foretaste of the interior decoration.

Interior – The castle was laid out as a series of bachelor apartments with **Winter and Summer Smoking Rooms, Bedroom and Bathroom**. The theme of the extraordinarily ornate decorative scheme is the passing of time, expressed in stained glass, polychrome sculptures, murals and lavish use of colour and gilt in a profusion of detail not quickly absorbed.

A ceiling devil guards the entrance while hounds of Hell bay in the floor, and the eccentric Burges' fondness for parrots finds expression in a doorhandle. A motto proclaims *Omnia vincit Amor* but, as Bute married in 1872, he can have had only a short time to enjoy these bachelor amenities before the focus of Castle life shifted to the **Nursery**, with its frieze of tales from the Brothers Grimm, Hans Andersen, and the Arabian Nights.

The most startling of all Burges' creations is perhaps the **Arab Room**, built into the 16C Herbert Tower, a reverie in marble and cedarwood of Andalusian ease and luxury, with a ceiling which is a *tour de force* of geometrical complexity.

A similar ceiling graces the **Dining Room**, one of a suite of rooms in the Bute Tower begun in 1872. Vice is defeated by Virtue in the **Sitting Room**, while in the **Bedroom** great play is made with the Marquess's first name, John, and 60 types of marble adorn the **Bathroom** behind its walnut screen.

The tower is capped by the **Roof Garden** with its fountain and peristyle, an evocation of Pompeii or Provence.

In the Beauchamp Tower, elaborate homage is paid in the **Chaucer Room** to the author of the Canterbury Tales, while above the **Banqueting Hall** with its great timber ceiling and depictions of episodes from the castle's history is the **Library**, its reading desks equipped with central heating.

The Castle houses two **military museums (BZ M1)** with well presented displays on the history of the Welch Regiment, founded in 1719, and of the 1st The Queen's Dragoon Guards.

■ Civic centre★ (BY)

The broad avenues, formal layout and grandiose public buildings of Cardiff's Civic Centre constitute an example of Beaux Arts planning more characteristic of Washington DC or Continental capitals than of Great Britain. As the city expanded rapidly in the latter part of the 19C the need became pressing for both open space and for new accommodation for administrative, civic and cultural functions.

The principal attraction for tourists is the splendidly refurbished **National Museum (BY)** but the whole precinct is worth exploring as a unique example of late-19C urban design.

Cathays Park (BY), just to the northeast of the castle, belonged to the Bute family who had laid out a central carriage drive through it, the forerunner of today's King Edward VII Avenue. The park was acquired by the City Council in 1898, and for nearly a century has been slowly filling up with structures designed to maintain the overall harmony of the site, nearly all of them in gleaming white Portland stone.

The **City Hall (BY H)**, less restrained in its design than the Museum, was completed in 1906 and its blend of Baroque more than adequately expresses the pride of a city growing in wealth and confidence. Fierce red dragons on pylons guard the approach, and another much bigger dragon perches on the dome, which itself is upstaged by the elaborately ornamented **clock tower** (194ft/59m high). Welsh heroes in marble grace the stairs, while the Council Chamber rises high into the dome.

The **Law Courts (BY)**, built in 1904, just to the west of City Hall, play in a minor key, compared to their flamboyant neighbour, and begin a run of buildings along King Edward VII Avenue. A neat little Classical pavilion of 1903/4 houses the University of Wales Registry. **Old County Hall (BY)** (1912) has an immensely imperious portico with broad steps and coupled Corinthian columns, while the former Technical College of 1916 is an exercise in severe neo-Grecian style. The **Welsh National Temple of Peace (BY)** in the stripped Classical style of the period was completed in 1938 and has an imposing hall in dove-grey marble and a crypt with a Book of Remembrance. The seat of central government in Wales is the **Welsh Office (BY)** of 1938, a plain building ornamented with the coats of arms of the then counties and vastly extended to the north by the less harmonious Crown Offices of 1980.

The spaciousness of the Civic Centre's layout is enhanced by the immaculately maintained flower beds and ornamental trees of **Alexandra Gardens (BY)**, whose centrepiece is the **Welsh National War Memorial (BY F)**. This temple-like structure, open to the sky, with its inscriptions in both Welsh and English, was erected in 1928 and adapted in 1949 to honour the dead of the Second World War.

To the east of the Gardens is the long and architecturally somewhat confused façade of **University College (BY)**.

■ National Museum and Gallery★★★ (BY)

The foundation stone of this great national institution occupying the southeastern corner of Cathays Park was laid in 1912. In gleaming white Portland stone like the other buildings of the Civic Centre, with a dome and with the words *AMGUEDDFA GENEDLAETHOL CYMRU* proudly inscribed above its entrance portal, it is a monumental structure, entirely worthy of the high purpose spelled out for it by its founders "to teach the world about Wales and to teach the Welsh people about their own Fatherland". Of the eight branches of the National Museum, this is by far the most important, a treasure house of art and archeology, science and natural history, with a reach, particularly in its wonderful painting collections, which goes far beyond the borders of the Principality. A major programme of refurbishment and extension, begun in 1989, has been carried to a triumphant conclusion, not only giving much-needed extra space but enhancing the visitor's appreciation of the grandeur of the calm and dignified interior.

Main Hall – Steps of Cornish granite lead into this superlative space, rising 85ft/26m from the extensive marble floor to the inside of the dome. Staircases at either end, lit by secondary domes, lead to the first floor balconies, which in turn give on to the galleries housing the art collection. Facing the entrance is the figure of an 18C drummer boy, part of the city's Boer War memorial, while an array of museum shops is sited discreetly behind columns and pilasters. A side door near the eastern stairway leads to a two-storey gallery with botanical displays.

Evolution of Wales★★ – Most of the Museum's ground-floor space is devoted to highly effective, state-of-the-art displays which evoke Wales' 4 600 million-year journey through time, from its original position south of the

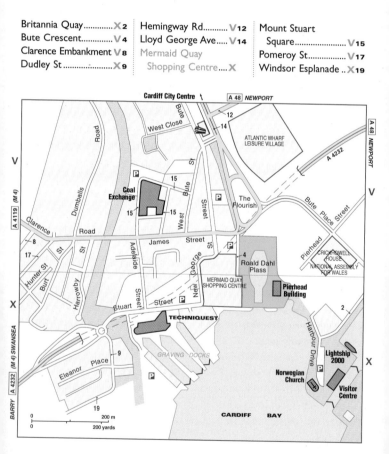

Equator to its present location. Geological processes are brought vividly to life by means of film and video presentations, while mineral specimens, far from lying inertly in cases, are revealed in all their glittering beauty and intrinsic fascination. Complex and convincing simulations portray ancient landscapes like the Carboniferous forest, basis of the country's former coal wealth, or the Triassic desert with its dinosaur denizens. The universe begins with an appropriately Big Bang, while volcanoes roar and splutter to an audience sitting on a (cool) lava flow, and a mammoth and its calf lumber ponderously around the mouth of an Ice Age cavern. The final gallery presents a scintillating selection of life forms and minerals illustrating the glorious diversity of the natural world, while the variety of Welsh habitats and scenery are the subject of further displays and elaborate simulations; a winter wind blasts through an oakwood, while shoreline and bird-rich cliff are dominated by a wide-jawed basking shark. Beyond, a dimly-lit sea-cavern echoes to the mysterious song of the whales.

Pottery and Porcelain* – The museum's collection of 18C porcelain is one of the richest in the world. Work from the great factories of continental Europe, Sèvres, Hochst, Vienna, and above all Meissen, is displayed on the north balcony, complemented by fine pieces from Chelsea, Derby and Worcester opposite. The Joseph Gallery gives a particularly full and fascinating account of the development of ceramics between 1764 and 1922 in the South Wales factories of Swansea, Nantgawr, Glamorgan and Llanelli. One landing showcase has a single superb Vienna bowl (c 1815-17) with colours of great luminosity; another, by contrast, has examples of modern work. More ceramics, along with other decorative art works, are displayed throughout the splendidly refurbished picture galleries in a remarkably effective way.

Art Galleries** – The galleries give a coherent survey of European painting and sculpture from the Renaissance onwards. British, particularly Welsh, art is strongly represented, but the museum's greatest glory is the Davies' collection of late-19C French art, which includes an array of Impressionist and other pictures of rare quality.

Archeology and Numismatics – The story of early people in Wales is told in some detail in upper rooms, with displays from the museum's rich archeological collections supplemented by models and other visual aids.

■ Cardiff Bay*

The historic dockland, typical of many harbour cities which reached their zenith in the 19C, is being renovated by an ambitious programme of conservation and restoration, and the creation of major new cultural and other facilities in a prestigious waterside setting.

The spectacular rise of the port of Cardiff really began when the **Second Marquess of Bute** financed the construction of what became Bute West Dock in 1839 and promoted the building of **Butetown**. Although conceived as a residential area, this 19C New Town came to rival the old city centre, with offices and commercial buildings as well as housing for all classes. As the port prospered, with the construction of ever more capacious docks to the east, moneyed folk moved out to leafy suburbs, replaced by a cosmopolitan population drawn in by the seaways from all quarters of the globe, and the area acquired its unofficial name of Tiger Bay. The gardens in the centre of the planned development of **Mount Stuart Square** were swept away to make room for the huge neo-Renaissance pile of the **Coal Exchange (V)**, completed in 1886. Millionaires rubbed shoulders on its trading floor in the decades when the world's appetite for Welsh steam coal seemed insatiable; after the First World War, coal began to give way to oil; the last deal was struck on the floor of the Exchange in 1958. The key to the revitalised waterside is the **barrage** (0.75mi/1km long), stretching from Queen Alexandra Dock in the east to Penarth Head in the west and creating a non-tidal freshwater lake (500 acres/200ha) with a waterfront (8mi/13km long) which provides a setting for an array of new developments, including shops and restaurants in Mermaid Quay. Some – like the controversial **Opera House** intended to be an inspiring new home for the internationally acclaimed Welsh National Opera company and a dedicated building for the National Welsh Assembly – are still at the planning stage.

Cardiff Bay Visitor Centre (X) – The overall vision for the waterside area can best be appreciated by a visit to the glittering quayside tube which houses the Centre and its enthusiastic presentation of the project.

Lightship 2000 (X) – The lightship, resplendent in red paint, was formerly known as Helwick LV14 and last stationed off the Gower Peninsula to warn shipping off the Helwick Swatch, a dangerous sand bank. It has conserved its equipment but has been refurbished to operate as a floating Christian Centre in Cardiff Bay.

Techniquest* (X) – Beside the old graving docks stands a striking structure of steel and glass. Under its barrel vault it contains 160 hands-on exhibits intended to make the appreciation of scientific principles an enjoyable and stimulating experience. Often thronged with school parties, Techniquest is equally fascinating for adults; it is quite possible to spend the greater part of a day here in enthusiastic interaction.

Pierhead Building (X) – In fierce red terracotta and brick and with a wealth of ornamental detail, this wonderfully self-assured landmark in French Gothic style was intended to impress all those arriving in the port. It was completed in 1896 by an associate of William Burges who had assisted in the transformation of Cardiff Castle, and originally housed the offices of the Bute Dock Company. Its dominance of the waterfront is now contested by the impressive St David's Hotel.

Norwegian Church (X) – This endearing little white-boarded structure in "Carpenter's Gothic", the first of its kind to be built (in 1868) outside Norway, was once the social and religious focus of the port's Norwegian community.

It was moved to this site and virtually rebuilt with the help of the children's author, **Roald Dahl**, who had been baptised in it. The building is now a café and small exhibition centre.

■ Excursion

Dyffryn Gardens★ – *8mi/13km west of city centre by A 48 and a minor road from the village of St Nicholas*

Though the Dyffryn estate can be traced back to the late Middle Ages, the present Dyffryn House is a late-19C mansion in French chateau style now used as a conference centre.

Its extensive grounds are a fine example of the work of the eminent Edwardian landscape architect **Thomas Mawson**, who collaborated with the owner, Reginald Cory, a keen horticulturalist and avid plant collector. ■

CARDIGAN

The former county town of Ceredigion (Cardiganshire) commands the lowest crossing point on the Teifi and has an air of importance out of all proportion to its modest size. The principal axis is formed by the handsome early-18C bridge, the ruined castle on its mound, and by the long, curving High Street which is mainly Victorian in character. At one time Cardigan was the second most significant port in Wales. Shipbuilding flourished in the 19C when more than 300 vessels were registered here. Most trade was coastal or with Ireland, but emigrant boats carried their human cargoes to Canada and the USA. The coming of railways and silting at the mouth of the estuary ended Cardigan's long history as a port, though

(Aberteifi) Ceredigion –
Population 3 815
Michelin Atlas p 24 or Map 503
G 27
Tourist Information Centre
– Theatr Mwldan, Bath
House Road, Cardigan
SA43 2JY ☎ 01239 613 230;
Fax 01239 613 600;
cardiganTIC@ceredigion; gov.uk

Out and About
Beaches – North at Mwnt, Aberporth, Tre-saith, Penbryn, Llangrannog and Cil Borth.

formal closure took place only in 1981, and the area downstream from the bridge known as **Castle Pool** still has old warehouses and something of a maritime character.

■ Excursions

Cilgerran Castle – *3mi/5km southeast by A 478 and a minor road.* Cilgerran's romantic situation on its crag high above the wooded gorge of the Teifi fascinated Turner, who made several studies of the castle in its setting, and the rugged ruin continues to exert its appeal today.

Welsh Wildlife Centre – *4mi/ 7km by A 478, minor road and rough track.* This extensive nature reserve is situated at the point where the Teifi emerges from its steep-sided wooded gorge and broadens out into an area of estuarine marshland. The habitats are exceptionally diverse, not only because of the change in the nature of the river but also because of the presence of old quarry workings, an abandoned railway line and a variety of relief forms carved by glacial meltwater channels.

Ceredigion Heritage Coast – *Access by side roads branching off northward from the A 487.* This splendid stretch of protected coastline runs east-northeastward from the tiny golfing resort of **Gwbert** on the Teifi estuary to New Quay Head, interrupted only by the town of Aberporth and its RAF station. Nearly all of it remains undeveloped. ■

© Wales Tourist Board

CAREW*

(Caeriw) Pembrokeshire

This pleasant little village stands at the crossing of the Carew River, one of the many tidal inlets penetrating deeply into the quiet countryside to the east of Milford Haven. Carew Castle broods over the broad pool that drove the village's tidal mill, the only one still intact in Wales. Nearby is a fine example of a Celtic Cross.

Michelin Atlas p 14 or Map 503 F 28

6mi/10km west of Tenby by B4318, A477 and A4075

Castle* – In this gentle landscape, the slight elevation of the castle site makes for a commanding position, and the defensive ditch guarding the approach to the stronghold was first dug in pre-Norman times, possibly as far back as the Iron Age. The present substantial ruins succeeded an earth-and-timber castle erected by the lord of Pembroke Castle, Gerald of Windsor, c 1100. Over a period of 400 years beginning in the late 12C, Carew evolved from a simple stone fortress to a palatial Tudor residence.

Carew Tidal Mill – *Walk from Castle car park (10min) or from National Park car park on north bank of millpond (5min).* The solid-looking four-storey mill building standing on the causeway probably dates from the very beginning of the 19C, though a mill was present on the site at least as early as Tudor times. Tidal mills had the advantage over wind and conventional water mills that their period of operation was predictable, varying only with the twice-daily rise and fall of the tide. Open sluices allowed the rising tide to fill the millpond (23 acres/9ha), the stored water then being released on the ebb to drive the pair of millwheels. This would mean frequent night shifts for the miller (one of whom at Carew was an Elizabeth Griffith). The mill worked until 1937, and older local people remember it rumbling and shuddering into the night. An audio-visual display gives a full account of the mill's history.

Carew Cross – *Close to Castle car park.* The wheel-head of this splendid cross is widely known as the aptly chosen symbol of CADW – Welsh Historic Monuments. The Cross (13ft/4m high) commemorates Maredudd ap Edwin, joint ruler of the western Welsh kingdom of Deheubarth until his death in battle in 1035. ■

52

CARMARTHEN

Well-placed on the rail and road routes to far southwestern Wales, the county town of Carmarthen is the market centre for much of this predominantly agricultural region, its daily bustle intensified when the thrice-weekly livestock market is under way.

The town has never hestitated to renew itself but a number of fragments remain of its 2000-year history, literally, in the case of the oak tree associated with Merlin the Enchanter, which was removed to make way for a road-widening scheme and now consists of a few shards preserved in the Civic Centre.

Under the Romans, Carmarthen, then the tribal capital of the Demetae, became **Moridunum**, the westernmost Roman settlement in Wales, with a large **amphitheatre**, capable of seating up to 5 000 spectators, which is now a public park. The layout of the Roman town is preserved in the modern street pattern to the east of St Peter's Church.

The Normans preferred to site their **castle** on a rocky knoll directly overlooking the River Tywi; it was sacked by Llywelyn the Great, rebuilt by John Nash and

(Caerfyrddin) Carmarthenshire
– Population 12 247
Michelin Atlas p 15 or Map 503
H 28
Tourist Information Centre – 11
Lammas Street, Carmarthen
SA31 3AQ
☎ *01267 231 557;*
Fax 01267 221 901; carmarthen
TIC@carmarthenshire.gov.uk

then again by the County Council in something of the manner of a French château. The 14C twin-towered **gatehouse** survives.

Below the castle, and quite separate from the Welsh borough to the east, an Anglo-Norman town grew up; its pleasingly intricate layout of streets and alleyways forms the core of the present town centre with the handsome Georgian **Guildhall** as its focal point.

Craft Centres – Merlin's Gallery, **Oriel Myrddin**, *(on the northern edge of the centre, opposite St Peter's Church)* has interesting displays of contemporary sculpture, crafts and paintings, many by local artists, arranged on the ground floor of the School of Art. Over 100 makers contribute to the display in **Origin Dyfed Gallery** *(1 St Mary's Street, off Guildhall Square).*

Gwili Pottery *(3mi/5km north in Pontarsais by A 484 and B 4301)* specialises in handthrown and individually decorated ceramics.

■ Excursions

Llansteffan Castle – *8mi southwest of Carmarthen by B 4312. Car park in village or by beach; 30min on foot return, partly up steep hill.* Llansteffan defends the approach to Carmarthen up the tidal Tywi, just as Laugharne Castle commands the estuary of the Taf.

The glorious **panorama** over the estuary and the surrounding country confirms the strategic significance of the site. To the north, it is clear how the village of Llansteffan has spread from the original nucleus around the church with its Pembrokeshire-style tower down the slope to its fine sandy beach.

Gwili Railway – *3mi/5km north of Carmarthen by A 484 and B 4301.* From Carmarthen the Great Western Railway meandered northward through the pretty valley of the River Gwili towards Newcastle Emlyn and Aberystwyth. The line was closed in 1973, but a section (1.5mi/2.5km long) has been reopened by enthusiasts, with steam and, only rarely, diesel passenger-carrying trains.

National Botanic Garden of Wales★ – *8mi/13km east by A 48 or B 4300 and B 4310.* The adaptation of the extensive 18C estate of **Middleton Hall** into a modern botanic garden is an unusual and exciting project. Water is an important element in the design – the main feature of the string of five lakes which are being restored with lakeside walks; a refreshing trickle winding its way down the **Broad Walk** in a pebbled channel; the subject of study in the Water Discovery Centre. The **Great Glasshouse**, a monster oval glass dome, houses a Mediterranean landscape bisected by a ravine – palm trees, cacti and a dragon tree.

Paxton's Tower – *8mi/13km east by B 4300; in Llanarthne turn right opposite the Paxton Arms; then take first left.* This huge triangular structure with its battlemented corner towers is one of the most grandiose follies in Great Britain. It has a magnificent prospect north over the meandering River Tywi. The folly was built in 1808 by Samuel Cockerell for Sir William Paxton of Middleton Hall, ostensibly to commemorate Nelson. ■

CASTELL COCH**

Cardiff

The once coal-blackened but increasingly clear Taff approaches Cardiff and the sea through a dramatic wooded gorge, once guarded by the red sandstone castle (Castell Coch = Red Castle) built by Gilbert de Clare in the latter part of the 13C. By the mid 19C de Clare's stronghold had long since crumbled into ruin, and the astonishing silhouette of high walls and conical towers rising through the trees today is the fanciful creation of the coal magnate Lord Bute and his equal in enthusiasm for the Middle Ages, the architect **William Burges** (1827-81).

The Butes' immense fortune had been accumulated through exploitation of coal-rich estates and the far-sighted development of the port of Cardiff. Though continuing to pursue his commercial interests, John, the Third Marquess of Bute (1847-1900), was more interested in immersing himself in the romantic vision he shared with Burges, who, by the late 1860s, was helping him in the transformation of his residence, Cardiff Castle, into

Michelin Atlas p 16 or Map 503 K 29 – 5mi/8km northwest of Cardiff

something more medieval than the Middle Ages themselves. The ruins of Castell Coch suggested themselves as a "country residence for occasional occupation in the summer", and Burges began work on the imaginative rebuilding of his master's second castle in 1871.

Exterior – Burges' reconstruction stands on the foundations of the original castle, whose sloping walls can best be appreciated from immediately below. Though the architect claimed authenticity for his designs, the exotic outline of his castle with its conical towers and elaborate roof shapes suggests Continental European precedents like the Château de Chillon rather than more local models.

Interior – The paved courtyard, with close-up views of the castle's elaborate roofline, steep steps and covered galleries, has served as a most satisfactory set for a number of swashbuckling films. ■

CHEPSTOW ★

Proclaiming itself the "first historic town in Wales", Chepstow stands on the Monmouthshire-Gloucestershire border, commanding the lower reaches of the tidal Wye just before it flows into the mighty Severn. The strategic importance of the site was recognised by the Norman William Fitz Osbern, the first builder of the splendid castle on its limestone spur high above the great bend of the Wye.

(Cas-Gwent) Monmouthshire – Population 9 461
Michelin Atlas p 16 or Map 503 L 29
Tourist Information Centre – Bridge Street, Chepstow NP16 5EY
☎ 01291 623 772; Fax 01291 628 004; chepstow-tic@tsww.com

■ Castle ★★

The castle is one of the most dramatically sited in Britain, particularly when first seen from the old main road descending to the river. Masonry merges with limestone cliff, making it difficult to distinguish the work of Man from that of Nature. Fitz Osbern came here in 1067, barely a year after the Norman conquest, erecting the hall keep known as the **Great Tower**, one of the very first stone castles built by the Normans in Britain and modelled on prototypes like Falaise in Normandy. Just over a century later, the castle was inherited by William Marshal, "the flower of chivalry" and builder of the great round keep at Pembroke. He and his sons strengthened Chepstow, rebuilding the walls of the Middle Bailey and adding the Lower and Upper Baileys as well as the Barbican at the furthermost western point of the ridge. The last major additions were those ordered by Roger Bigod III, who held the castle from 1270 to 1306; they included the suites of rooms overlooking the Wye on the north side of the Lower Bailey and the massive tower named after Henry Marten, one of the signatories of Charles I's death warrant, who was held prisoner here for 20 years.

The castle's formidable defences made it one of the few which Owain Glyn Dŵr refrained from attacking; in the Civil War it was held for the King (twice) and surrendered to Parliament (also twice).

Chepstow Museum – The local museum occupies the rooms of an exceptionally fine 18C town mansion which once belonged to a prosperous local merchant and apothecary. Its excellent displays give a thorough account of Chepstow's past as a port, shipbuilding centre and market town.

Chepstow Bridge – The elegant cast-iron bridge was built in 1816 to a design based on the work of John Rennie. It no longer bears the burden of main road traffic owing to the construction of a bypass to the south, which crosses the Wye next to the railway bridge originally built by Brunel for the South Wales Railway.

Town Gate and Portwall – From the late 13C Chepstow was protected by **walls**, which because of the hilly nature of the town site enclosed a large unbuilt area of orchards and open spaces. Several stretches remain.

■ Excursions

Wynd Cliff★ – *2.5mi/4km north by A 466 and a minor road; from car park 20min on foot return.* The densely wooded limestone cliffs of the gorge rise here to a height of 800ft/240m. From the giddy **Eagle's Nest viewpoint** at the top of the cliff, the eye ranges over the winding Wye, the great bridges over the Severn, and the English counties beyond.

Severn Crossing – One of the most splendid of rivers, the tidal Severn (Hafren in Welsh) was for long a barrier to easy communication between the west of England and South Wales, not least because of its astonishing **tidal range** (up to 46ft/14m).

A **railway tunnel** was built in 1886 between the English shore and Caldicot, but until well into the second half of the 20C road traffic either went via Gloucester many miles upstream or waited for one of the little **ferries** linking Beachley and Aust.

Bridging the broad estuary presented many problems; the high-energy tidal regime causes fast and unpredictable currents, and the rock foundation is fissured, faulted and water-bearing.

© Wales Tourist Board

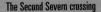
The Second Severn crossing

Work finally began on the magnificent road **suspension bridge** carrying the M4 motorway in 1961 and it was opened in 1966. It is used by some 50 000 vehicles a day and also by cyclists and pedestrians; tolls are levied on westbound traffic only. The main span is 3 400ft/1 036m in length and the towers are 445ft/146m high. Quite distinct from the main suspension bridge is the more modest but still considerable stayed-girder structure carrying traffic over the Wye.

The capacity of the bridge was soon exceeded, and inconvenience is caused by restrictions placed on its use because of high winds and maintenance operations. Vigorous lobbying, particularly by South Wales industrial and commercial interests, led to studies of alternative additional crossings, including a tunnel. A second bridge was the preferred option. The **Second Severn Crossing** is sited downstream from the suspension bridge so that it does not spoil the magnificent outline of the former. This new bridge (nearly 3mi/5km long) has as its main span a cable-stayed bridge (1 500ft/450m) approached by viaducts with spans of varying length.

Caldicot Castle and Country Park – 6mi/10km west of Chepstow by M 4, exit Junction 23 (signs). Credit is due to the Victorian barrister and antiquarian, Joseph Cobb, for the survival of this handsome medieval monument. Rejecting the 19C fashion for ivy-clad ruins, he set about the meticulous excavation and restoration of the castle, which was begun by the Normans in the 10C. A stereotaped tour guides visitors around the gritstone tower, which has fine views of the River Severn, and round the Woodstock Tower, which was named after Thomas of Woodstock, who was betrayed by his nephew Richard II and murdered. The gatehouse is particularly impressive; it has fine masonry and a half-timbered upper storey, added by Cobb.

Penhow Castle★ – 7mi/11km west of Chepstow by A 48 or M 4, exit at junction 24. By the mid 20C this delectable fortified manor house had become little more than an appendage to a farm. Since 1973 it has been restored and refurnished with ingenuity and enthusiasm to give a fascinating insight into the evolution of a squire's residence from crude keep to country house.

Penhow was one of a number of smaller Norman strongholds built in a buffer zone around the mighty castle at Chepstow to warn of any impending Welsh attack. It probably dates from the start of the 12C. The builder of its three-storey **keep** was a member of the Anglo-Norman family, de Saint Maur, who became known as the Seymours and who eventually provided a queen for Henry VIII. The site, a rocky knoll, overlooks what was the main road into South Wales. ■

FISHGUARD

Three settlements stand by the shore of Fishguard Bay. **Lower Town** (y Cwm), hemmed in by cliffs at the mouth of the Gwaun valley, is the original fishing village, with seafarers' cottages and a small number of fishing boats as well as pleasure craft. **Fishguard** proper on the clifftop has many of the facilities of a larger town, while on the far, western side of the bay is the village of **Goodwick** together with the railway and modern harbour with its roll-on roll-off ferry service to Ireland. ∎

(Abergwaun) Pembrokeshire – Population 3 128
Michelin Atlas p 14 or Map 503 F 28
Tourist Information Centres – Town Hall, The Square, Fishguard SA65 9HA
☎ 01348 873 484; Fax 01348 875 246.
2 Bank Cottages, Long Street, Newport SA42 0TN
☎ 01239 820 912; Fax 01239 820 912.

© Wales Tourist Board

Out and About
Craft Centres – **Fishguard Invasion Centre** (St Mary's Church Hall, Main Street) displays an **embroidered tapestry** commemorating the French invastion in 1797 and also work by local artists and craftspeople.
Beaches – At Strumble Head (west) and at Cwm-yr-eglwys and Newport Sands North (east).

GLAMORGAN HERITAGE COAST★

Vale of Glamorgan

The Vale of Glamorgan faces the Bristol Channel from a splendid stretch of cliffs (13mi/20km) which extend westward from the great power stations at Aberthaw to the little resort of Ogmore-by-Sea. The Heritage Coast, designated in 1972, extends further west to take in the dunes of Merthyr Mawr and Newton Point. The cliffs (average height 100ft/30m) are composed of alternate layers of Liassic limestones and shales which are continually being eroded by the sea and thus present a constant vertical or overhanging profile. The beach normally con-

Michelin Atlas pp 15 and 16 or Map 503 J 29
Tourist Information Centres – Town Hall, Llantwit Major, ✆/Fax 01446 796 086;
Heritage Coast Visitor Centre, Southerndown near Ogmore-by-Sea,
✆ *01656 880 157; Fax 01656 880 931; heritagecoast@highways.valeofglamorgan.gov.uk*

Blue Anchor Pub, Aberhaw

sists of a level platform of plates of limestone, sometimes with a band of pebbles at the cliff foot. The great tidal range (up to 50ft/15m) of the Bristol Channel, together with the risk of cliff falls, make the shore a potentially perilous environment.

A number of Iron-Age forts, now much eroded, were built along the clifftop, notably at **Summerhouse Point** and **Nash Point**. Rather than looking to the sea, the medieval population settled just inland, farming the rich soils of the Vale and leaving a series of pretty **villages** with houses and churches built from the blue-grey limestone.

Llantwit Major-Llanilltud Fawr – This attractive little town is the largest of the settlements fringing the coast, sited, like the others, well inland, and built of the local limestone. The place derives its name from Illtud, a late-5C Celtic saint, founder of the famous monastic college at which, by tradition, St David was educated. The renovated medieval **Town Hall** now houses an Information Centre on the Glamorgan Coast area. A maze of medieval streets occupies the low rise below which stands **St Illtud's Church**. This is an extraordinary structure, in effect two churches in one, linked by a slender tower. To the east is the 13C collegiate church, with a splendid wall-painting of a big-footed St Christopher, and a Jesse niche. To the west is the original parish church, Norman in date but sited on the foundations of the 6C Celtic church and largely rebuilt in the 15C. It houses a number of effigies as well as a fine collection of **early-Christian stones and crosses**, evidence of a school of sculpture which flourished here from the late 9C onwards. Further westward still are the remains of the Galilee Chapel.

St Donat's Castle – Embedded in woodland roughly midway along the coast is this much-restored castle, now the home of **Atlantic College**, one of a number of international sixth-form institutions which prepares students for the International Baccalaureate Diploma. Restoration of the castle began in the early 20C and was continued by the newspaper magnate Randolph Hearst, who re-roofed the dining hall with a ceiling from a Lincolnshire church. The **gardens** dropping steeply to the shore were first terraced in Tudor times. ■

Walks – A **clifftop walk** runs almost the whole length of the coast, giving continually changing views of the Channel and its shipping, and of the coast and hills of Somerset and Devon.
Beaches – At a number of places where breaks in the cliffline occur, including **Dunraven Bay**.

GOWER PENINSULA ★★

Swansea

With its magnificent coastline of dramatic cliffs and sweeping marshlands and its interior of ancient farmland and commons, this peninsula (14mi/22km long) projecting westward into Carmarthen Bay has been called a "microcosm of all that is finest in the Welsh landscape". Its designation in 1957 as Britain's first Area of Outstanding Natural Beauty gave official recognition to its special quality as well as offering it some protection against the spreading suburbs of Swansea at its eastern extremity.

Few contrasts could be greater than that between the formidable rocky ramparts of the Gower's southern coast and the vast expanses of sand dune, saltmarsh and mud which merge into the glittering estuary of the River Loughor to the north. The south shore attracts ramblers to its clifftop paths and myriad families to its glorious sandy bays, while surfers ride the curling breakers of westward-facing **Rhossili Bay**, one of the country's most spectacular beaches. The salty grass of the north coast is grazed by sheep and ponies, while its tidal mud provides rich sustenance for a wealth of seabirds no longer subjected to such intense competition by the famous cockle-gatherers of Crofty.

Michelin Atlas p 15 or Map 503 H 29
Tourist Information Centres – Gower Heritage Centre, Park Mill,
☎ 01792 371206; Fax 01792 371471; www.gowerheritagecentre.co.uk
Rhossili National Trust Visitor Centre, Coastguard Cottages, Rhossili,
☎ 01792 390707; rhossili@nationaltrust.org.uk

■ Sights

Oxwich – The splendid stretch of sand in this bay is backed by dunes and freshwater marshes.

Rhossili ★★ – The approach by road through the farmlands of the west-

© Wales Tourist Board

Out and About

Tide Timetable – For information about the times of high and low tides consult the display at the Rhossili National Trust Visitor Centre *(see above)* and Old Coastguard Station Visitor Centre or contact the Coastguard Tel 01792 366 534.

Beaches – At Caswell Bay, Port Eynon and Rhossili.

Exploring On Foot – There are several good points for leaving the car and taking to the footpaths *(listed in clockwise order from the western outskirts of Swansea)*:

– From the Gower Heritage Centre *(A 4118 – car park)* northwest through deciduous wood to **Park Wood** and the **Giant's Grave**, a prehistoric burial site;

– From Kittle Post Office *(B 4436)* walk south, descending a steep path to an old rocky river bed, where the water can be heard flowing underground;

– From the viewpoint above **Penmaen** *(car park, observation table and picnic site)* walk down to the bay, via stepping stones *(1.5mi)*;

– Explore the **Oxwich Bay National Nature Reserve** *(beach car park)* or take the woodland walk to **Oxwich Point**;

– From Pitton car park *(off B 4247)* walk along the cliffs between **Port Eynon** and **Rhossili**;

– Explore the **Whiteford National Nature Reserve** *(car park north of Llanmadog Church)* or walk up to the summit of **Cefn Bryn** for the view and **Arthur's Stone**.

Worms Head is accessible by a rocky causeway for only 2hr on either side of low tide.

Local Specialities – Sea trout (sewin), cockles (from Crofty on the north coast) and shellfish, laver bread (seaweed), marsh samphire and salt marsh lamb, mushrooms, gulls' eggs.

ern Gower does little to prepare the visitor for the scenic surprises of the peninsula's southwestern extremity. To the north, **Rhossili Down**, Gower's highest hill, drops seaward to a grassy platform one field wide, then via a low and shallow cliff to a broad bay curving northward to distant dunes and swept continuously by skeins of surf. To the south, beyond the narrow strips of the village's still-surviving medieval fields, a great sea-snake seems to undulate, raising its rocky head to scan the ocean. This is **Worms Head**, a mile-long limestone spit divided into three sections and accessible on foot. *See out and about above.* ■

GROSMONT

(Y Grusmwnt) Monmouthshire

A compact village like Grosmont is a rarity in this region of scattered farmsteads. The village was originally a medieval borough founded along with the castle above it. The little **Town Hall** in the main street is a somewhat for-lorn symbol of former municipal glories. The **Church of St Nicho-las**, with its eight-sided tower, do-minant spire and little-used nave, is obviously much too large for the present rural population.

Three castles fayre – The "Three castles fayre.... in a goodly ground" (Thomas Churchyard, 1587), which helped consolidate the Norman grip on the southern March, were Grosmont, White Castle and Sken-frith. The "goodly ground" is an apt description of the lovely, lonely farming countryside of northern Monmouthshire, cut by the wind-ing River Monnow and Offa's Dyke Footpath and undisturbed by main roads and modern intrusions.

Michelin Atlas p 16 or Map 503 L 28

Grosmont Castle – The castle stands protected by its moat above the Monnow. It owes much of its present appearance to Hubert de Burgh, a distinguished soldier of wildly fluctuating fortunes who was twice lord of the Three Cas-tles in the early 13C, and who built the hall block and improved the defences generally.

A century later, when the Three Castles had passed into the hands of the Earls of Lancaster, and the Welsh threat had been largely overcome, the role of Grosmont changed from fortress to favoured residence and remodelling took place in order to improve the level of comfort. The tall and el-egant Gothic chimney dates from this period.

The last time any of the Three Cas-tles saw action was in 1405 when the future Henry V beat off Owain Glyn Dŵr's rebels with great loss of life. ■

HAVERFORDWEST

Dominated by the ruins of its Norman castle, the old county town of Pembrokeshire still has a townscape marked by the rebuilding that took place in Georgian times, though little remains in today's workaday town of the atmosphere of what, at its height, was called a "little Bath".

Haverfordwest owes its importance to its position at what until the 1970s was the lowest crossing point of the Western Cleddau River. The rebuilding of the castle in stone in the 12C-13C was followed by urban expansion, first in the form of a Flemish settlement around the Church of St Martin, then by a walled and gated town on the river bank below the castle. Trade by sea with France, Spain and Ireland as well as with other British ports made Haverfordwest "the best buylt, the most civill occupied town in South Wales" by Tudor times. The coming of the railway, however, slowly strangled this traffic, although it was not until the 1920s that the last small steamer sailed away down the river. The maritime past is recalled by a few old warehouses and the *Bristol Trader Inn* on the west bank of the river, while the old dock on the east bank has been ignominiously filled in to create a car park.

*(Hwlffordd) Pembrokeshire
– Population 11 099
Michelin Atlas p 14 or Map 503
F 28
Tourist Information Centre
– Old Bridge, Haverfordwest,
Pembrokeshire SA61 2EZ
☎ 01437 763 110; Fax 01437
767 738.*

Scolton Museum and Country Park★ – *4mi/7km north of Haverfordwest by B 4329.* The 19C house known as Scolton Manor has been refurbished to evoke the era at the turn of the 19C-20C. Visitors can wander through the family rooms, servants' parlour and extensive cellars; on the first floor are the nursery and a costume gallery on the theme of "Victorian Vogue". The stable block now houses displays on farriery, carpentry and ironmongery; another outbuilding is devoted to an exhibition on Pembrokeshire railways.

There is a nature trail in the parkland and a visitor centre with exhibits on "green" issues. ■

HAY-ON-WYE*

This little medieval market town on the English border emerged from the sleep of centuries in the 1960s when an eccentric and enterprising bookseller filled a fire station, cinema and empty shops with secondhand books. His lead was followed by other dealers, who have made Hay into a magnet for bibliophiles from around the world. The annual Literary Festival attracts many visitors; others use the town as their base for exploring the magnificent landscapes of the Wye Valley and the Black Mountains.

Town Centre – Cognate with the French *haie* and the Dutch *Den Haag,* Hay signifies a place surrounded by an enclosure. The town's original nucleus lies just to

(Y Gelli) Powys – Population 1 407
Michelin Atlas pp 25 and 26 or Map 503 K 27

the southwest, where the parish church – a 19C rebuilding – stands close to the original castle mound of the early 12C. This first Norman fortress was replaced c 1200 by the present **castle** rising over the close-packed streets. It was sacked by Welsh and English in turn, and now consists of keep and gateway and the many-gabled Jacobean mansion inserted into the ruins c 1660. The mansion was burnt out in 1977 and is slowly being restored; some of its outbuildings, inevitably so in Hay, house antiquarian books.

The Book King

Since Richard Booth came to Hay in 1961, his book empire has waxed, then waned. The original cinema bookshop is now run by a rival, but Booth's books are still piled high in "The Famous", a labyrinth of a building behind an exuberant Victorian shopfront featuring carved heads of bulls and other beasts. Never slow to promote himself or his adopted cause of rural revival, Booth has remained in the public eye over the years by having himself crowned as the King of Hay, declaring independence from both Wales and Great Britain, and issuing his own, edible banknotes (printed on rice paper).

Castle and mansion are built in warm grey stone, as is much of the rest of the town. The overall character of the buildings lining the complex web of streets and alleyways seems Victorian and late Georgian, though in many cases more ancient structures lie hidden behind later façades. The oldest building is a 16C cruck-built hall, now the *Three Tuns* public house. The three town gates have long since disappeared but the triangular outline of the walls can still be traced and some fragments remain to northeast and southwest.

The town seems to turn its back on the River Wye, from which it is separated by the course of the 18C horse-drawn tramway and the 19C railway which succeeded it but which was itself closed in the 1960s.

■ Excursion

Hay Bluff ★★– *4mi/6km south of Hay-on-Wye, mostly on a single track road.* The spectacular north-facing escarpment of the Black Mountains, visible from as far away as the Cotswold Hills (some 50mi/80km to the east) can be appreciated in close-up from the sweeping stretch of open land known as Hay Common or the Allt. The narrow road traverses the common, grazed by wandering sheep and ponies, and winds up to Gospel Pass (1 778ft/542m). ■

© Wales Tourist Board

LLANCAIACH FAWR MANOR *

Caerphilly

Restored and opened to the public, this severe grey-stone manor house in the Rhymney Valley offers its visitors an entertaining and completely convincing experience of the life led within its walls at the time of the Civil War (1642-49).

The house occupies the site of a medieval dwelling, and was begun in the early 16C for the Pritchard (ap Richard) family. With thick walls (4ft/1.22m), small windows

Michelin Atlas p 16 or Map 503 K 29

which could not be opened, and narrow, easily defended staircases, it was meant to resist all but the most determined attack, with an east wing capable of being sealed off from the remainder of the house. 17C improvements included the construction of a grand staircase and the laying out of a formal walled garden. ■

LLANDAFF CATHEDRAL *

Cardiff

Now one of the more refined suburbs of Cardiff, village-like Llandaff with its Green, Bishop's Palace and ancient cathedral was once a borough in its own right.

The cathedral was begun under the Normans in 1120 by Bishop Urban and added to in the 13C and 14C, while the **Jasper Tower** was built in 1485 as a replacement for the older belltower whose ruins

Michelin Atlas p 16 or Map 503 K 29 – 2mi/3km northwest of Cardiff city centre

can still be seen on the Green. Serious restauration began in the 1830s and an equivalent effort had to be made after the Second World War to make good the extensive damage caused by the Luftwaffe in 1941. ■

LLANDEILO ★

A hilltop site above the Tywi, a magnificent stone bridge, a pleasing assemblage of Georgian and Victorian buildings, and proximity to the ancient parklands of **Dinefwr Castle** give Llandeilo an air of importance out of all proportion to its present diminutive size.

From its bluff, the town overlooks the confluence of the Tywi and Cennen at a point where the main valley narrows and forms a crossing point. The 6C Celtic **Saint Teilo** founded a monastery here, which however was in decline by the 9C. A settlement continued in existence, even outlasting the rival Welsh and English boroughs planted to the west, which had disappeared by about the 15C. The Welsh borough had grown up around Dinefwr Castle, built on another rocky bluff just to the west of Llandeilo.

Llandeilo is best approached from the south, across the many-arched **bridge** with its imposing central span (145ft/44m), which in 1848 replaced an earlier more modest structure. The bridge approach climbs the hill towards the town, shouldering aside the older houses which still mark the alignment of the old road. At the top of the

Carmarthenshire – Population 850
Michelin Atlas p 15 or Map 503 I 28
Tourist Information Centre – Crescent Road Car Park, Llandeilo SA19 6HN
☎ 01558 824 226; Fax 01558 824 252.

hill the highway cuts through the churchyard of the large **Church of St Teilo**, its military-looking tower dating from the 13C but the rest of it a rebuilding by Sir Giles Gilbert Scott in 1850.

Dinefwr Park★ – *Restoration in progress*. This is one of the finest landscape parks in Wales; it and its two great buildings, **Dinefwr castle** and its more domesticated replacement, **Newtown House**, are the object of conservation.

■ Excursions

Carreg Cennen Castle★ – *4mil 7km southeast of Llandeilo by A 483 and minor roads and on foot across a field*. On its wild and wind-torn crag overlooking the little River Cennen as it tumbles down from the Black Mountain, this ruined fortress rarely fails to stir the imagination. ■

LLANELLI

For centuries the few inhabitants of what is now the largest town in Carmarthenshire lived from farming and fishing, though by the 16C they had begun, as Leland noted, not only to "digge coales" but to ship them out, first from the banks of the tidal River Loughor at Ysbyty, then from a growing complex of wharves and docks to the south of the present town centre. Coal exports began to decline as early as the mid 19C, but by then Llanelli had become a leading centre of metalworking, especially of the **tinplate** production which has continued until the present day. The town's passion is Rugby football, focused on the fortunes of the home team, the *Scarlets*, whose resounding anthem, *Sospan Fach*, is in fact no more than a ditty about a little saucepan.

Llanelli's rapid industrial growth in the 19C obliterated most traces of its past, and the dominant element in today's townscape consists of variations on the theme of the Victorian terraced house. The busy town centre with its market is mostly pedestrianised and has recently received a much-needed refurbishment.

The **Millennium Coastal Park**, opened in 2000, forms a green

Carmarthenshire — Population 74 698
Michelin Atlas p 15 or Map 503 H 28
Tourist Information Centre — Public Library, Vaughan Street, Llanelli SA15 3AS
☎ *01554 772 020; Fax 01554 750 125.*

belt (14mi/22km), along the seashore, between Machynys (south of Llanelli) and Pembrey, a chain of gardens and woodlands, wetlands and fishing lakes, dunes, quays and harbours, linked by a footpath and cycleway, offering a variety of facilities — water sports centre, outdoor and indooor events areas and an 18-hole golf course.

Kidwelly Castle★ – *9mi/15km northwest of Llanelli by A 484 and Kidwelly bypass.* On its ridge overlooking the limit of tidal water on the River Gwendraeth, Kidwelly (Cydweli) was one of a chain of Norman castles intended to secure the coastal route to the west. Roofless, but otherwise well preserved, it conveys a most satisfying impression of a medieval stronghold, especially when its splendid array of walls and towers is viewed from the far bank of the river. ∎

LLANTHONY PRIORY★★

Monmouthshire

The noble ruin of this Augustinian priory shelters in the Vale of Ewyas, a secluded valley winding up to Gospel Pass on the northern edge of the Black Mountains. Though English Herefordshire lies on the far side of the high moorland ridge to the east, this is one of the remotest, and most delectable, of all the monastic sites in Wales.

Priory Ruins – The priory stands

Michelin Atlas pp 16 and 25 or Map 503 K 28

on a level shelf of land a little above the emerald meadows and dark alders which accompany the course of the Honddu. To the northeast, the slopes rising steeply to the high moors are studded with the larches and chestnuts planted by Landor as part of his misconceived scheme to recreate a deer park. ■

MARGAM PARK★

Neath Port Talbot

Comprising the remains of a great Cistercian abbey, the country's longest orangery and a huge and ruined neo-Tudor mansion, the vast domain of Margam is today a country park with a whole array of visitor attractions and an annual programme of events which draws in thousands.

Margam Castle – The building is a Tudor-Gothic fantasy of bays, gables, pinnacles and turrets, centred on a great octagonal tower, easier

Michelin Atlas p 15 or Map 503 I 29

perhaps to appreciate as a partial ruin than to live in.

Orangery★ – This splendid structure (327ft/100m long) is built in Classical style, its succession of round-headed windows terminated at either end by pedimented pavilions. It has been adapted for use as a banqueting hall with the judicious insertion of a glass screen to preserve the long internal vista. ■

MERTHYR TYDFIL

High up in the Taff Vale, this bleak town was for many years the "Iron Capital of the World", sending its products all over the rapidly industrialising 19C globe. As metal manufacture moved elsewhere, coal mining became the principal activity. Now that too has gone, replaced in part by new light industries. Enough of the early industrial heritage remains, however, to evoke both the vigour and squalor of Merthyr's past.

Cyfarthfa Castle Museum – The pseudo-medieval stronghold of 1825 overlooks the valley with the long-abandoned site of the Cyfarthfa ironworks which provided the funds for its construction. The castle was built in 1825 by Richard Lugar for William Crawshay II; it had 72 rooms in which the families of successive "Iron Kings" were able to live a lavish lifestyle. As well as the usual 19C conifers and bedding displays, the extensive grounds (160 acres/67ha) also included an ice-house and a "pinery" for pineapple production; it was the head gardener's boast that he could produce a hundred pineapples for Christmas dinner! The lake, which also supplied water to the works, was liable to leak, and in the end cost as much as the house to construct.

(Merthyr Tudful) Merthyr Tydfil
– Population 59 317
Michelin Atlas p 16 or Map 503
J 28
Tourist Information Centre – 14a
Cleveland Street, Merthyr Tydfil
CF47 8AU
☎ 01685 379 884; Fax 01685 350 043.

Ynysfach Iron Heritage Centre – Built in 1836, this dignified structure in contrasting dark and light stone once housed the beam engine which supplied the blast for the adjoining furnaces. Derelict for many years, it now houses a museum which tells the story of iron-making in Merthyr, partly through an excellent audio-visual presentation. Among the objects on display are a number of decorative iron doorstops, including one showing the figure of George Washington.

■ Excursions

Elliot Colliery – 10mi/16km southeast by A 465 and A 469. The old Winding House contains the largest steam engine of its kind in Wales, a Thornhill and Wareham engine, later converted to compressed air and now operated by electricity. The semi-spiral diablo drum enabled one cage to be lowered as the other was raised. A small exhibition charts the history of the local coal industry, particularly Penallta Colliery.

Ebbw Vale – *10mi/16km east.* In 1938, with government assistance, one of the most modern steel plants in Europe was sited in this Depression-stricken town at the head of its valley. Respite was relatively short-lived; by 1978 the works had shut. Reclamation of the site began in 1986. One-and-a-half million cubic metres of slag was reshaped, 6 000kg of fertiliser spread and 1.8 million new trees, shrubs and flowers planted, and in 1992 one of Britain's National Garden Festivals was staged in these unlikely surroundings. The core of the **Festival Park** remains, with a **Festival Park Visitor Centre**, Oriental Pool, Mythical Beast, and Tropical Plant House, centrepiece of what it is hoped will become a dynamic development of new Home Counties-style housing and light industry.

Aneurin Bevan Memorial – This group of roughly-shaped standing stones erected on the breezy heights above Ebbw Vale commemorates Aneurin Bevan (1897-1960), who was born in Tredegar at the top of the Sirhowy Valley. He represented Ebbw Vale in Parliament for 30 years and was known as an eloquent orator; his lasting legacy is the British National Health Service, which he founded in 1948. ∎

Aneurin Bevin memorial

MONMOUTH ★

The old county town of Monmouthshire stands on a neck of land between the Wye and its tributary the Monnow, after which the town is named. Though the Romans had a garrison here, the story of urban Monmouth really began when the Normans built their castle on a steep rise above the Monnow and established a market settlement laid out along a broad street leading downhill to the river crossing. Despite setbacks caused by repeated flooding and the Black Death when parts of the town were abandoned, Monmouth seems to have enjoyed almost continuous prosperity.

Monmouth is associated with a number of famous figures. Of Breton descent, **Geoffrey of Monmouth** (b 1090) was responsible for the *Historia regnum Britanniae,* supposedly a translation "from the ancient British tongue" of a largely mythical history of Britain, which was one of the most popular books of the Middle Ages and is the basis of much of the Arthurian myth. By tradition, **Henry V** was born in Monmouth Castle in 1387.

Admiral **Lord Nelson** made the trip down the Wye in 1802, partly in order to report to the Admiralty on the state of that strategic

(Trefynwy) Monmouthshire – Population 8 204 Michelin Atlas p 16 or Map 503 L 28 Tourist Information Centre – Shire Hall, Agincourt Square, Monmouth NP5 3DY ☎ 01600 713 899; Fax 01600 772 794.

naval resource, the timber of the nearby Forest of Dean; both he and the town seem to have fallen for each other. **Charles Stuart Rolls** (1877-1910), who together with Henry Royce founded the firm which built the world's most prestigious motorcars, was born near the town. In 1896, while still an undergraduate, he took three days to drive from Cambridge to Monmouth in the first car ever to be seen in the county.

Agincourt Square – The old market square was given this historicising name in 1830 in an attempt to raise the town's profile among tourists making the fashionable picturesque journey down the Wye.

Castle and Great House – All that really remains of the Castle are the ruins of the Great Tower, built in the late 14C by John of Gaunt in order, it is thought, to provide a fit setting for the birth of his grandson, Henry V. ■

NEWPORT

The Norman lords of Wentloog appreciated Newport's strategic position as the lowest crossing point of the tidal River Usk, and began building their castle here in the early 14C. But Newport remained a modest market town until touched by the Industrial Revolution, when it became the outlet for the coal pits and metal works of the Eastern Valleys as well as an important engineering centre in its own right. What in 1801 was a village-sized population of 1 100 had swelled by the start of the 20C to 67 000. Now the third-largest city in Wales, Newport is a thriving shopping and commercial centre serving a wide region, seeking to repair the damage done by over-enthusiastic redevelopment in the 1960s and 1970s by more judicious, small-scale civic improvements and works of public art.

Museum and Art Gallery (AX M)* – *John Frost Square*. Recently refurbished and housed on several floors in the same modern building as the Public Library, this is one of the major museums and galleries of Wales, with much space given over to well-staged temporary exhibitions.

Newport Castle (AX) – Newport's original stronghold, a

*(Casnewydd) Newport
– Population 115 896
Michelin Atlas p 16 or Map 503
K 29
Tourist Information Centres
– John Frost Square, Newport
NP20 1PA;
☎ 01633 842 962; Fax 01633
222 615; newport-tic@tsww.com
First Services & Lodge, Junction
23A/M4, Magor NP6 3YL
☎ 01633 881 122; Fax 01633
881 985.*

motte-and-bailey castle on Stow Hill near today's cathedral, was abandoned in the mid 14C when a separate Norman lordship, Wentloog (Gwynllŵg), was carved out of Glamorgan. In its place, Hugh d'Audele began to construct a castle defending the river crossing. His fortress was both strengthened and made more habitable in the early and mid 15C but, after 1521 when its lord, the Third Duke of Buckingham, was beheaded, the building was neglected and by the 18C had fallen into ruin. The *coup de grâce* came when railway and canal promoters drove their schemes through the castle precincts with the utmost ruthlessness and part of the castle became a brewery. ■

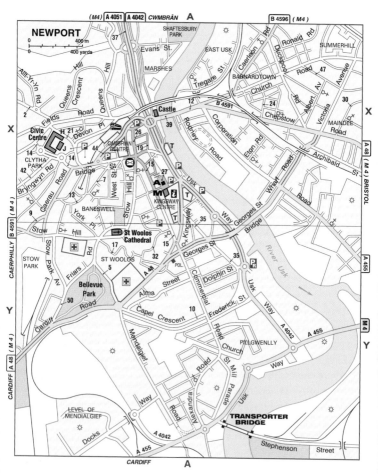

PEMBROKE**

The Normans based their operations in southwestern Wales on the castle and town laid out along a low and narrow limestone spur, once almost surrounded by an inlet from Milford Haven. Their mighty castle still stands, dominated by its great round keep and in turn dominating the town which, albeit rebuilt over the centuries, still retains its ancient street pattern and long burgage plots running down to the vestiges of the medieval walls.

(Penfro) Pembrokeshire
– Population 7 230
Michelin Atlas p 14 or Map 503
F 28
Tourist Information Centre
– Visitor Centre, Commons Road, Pembroke SA71 4EA
☎ 01646 622 388; Fax 01646 621 396.

Castle★★ – The castle was founded by Roger de Montgomery in 1093 and served the Normans well, never being taken by the Welsh and making an excellent base for campaigning in Ireland.

It owes its present form to the efforts of William Marshal, Earl of Pembroke 1189-1219, and those of his son, another William. Within the inner ward at the westernmost tip of the promontory, the first William expressed his power by raising the mighty round **keep** (50ft/15m in diameter and 75ft/23m high) with indestructible walls (19ft/6m thick at the base). This truly monumental structure, based on French practice, and almost unique in Britain, is crowned by a splendid stone dome, awe-inspiring when viewed from below. A lesser tower contains a sinister dungeon, while beneath the late-13C Great Hall with its Decorated windows is the extraordinary **Wogan Cavern**, opening out towards the northern arm of the inlet and probably used as a boathouse. Other structures in the inner ward include the remains of the Norman Hall, probably built at the same time as the Keep, the late 13C-early14C County Court, the Chapel, the Western Hall, and the Horseshoe Gate, the chief entrance until the outer ward was built.

The **Gatehouse**, almost a castle within a castle, is approached by a semicircular barbican. Inside the **Gatehouse Tower** are displays celebrating the role the castle played in English history as "The Seat of Earls" as well as a fine model clarifying the stages of its construction. ■

PEMBROKESHIRE COAST**

Pembrokeshire

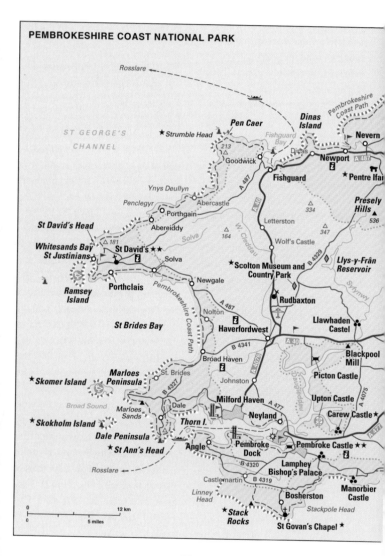

PEMBROKESHIRE COAST NATIONAL PARK

Rosslare

ST GEORGE'S CHANNEL

★ Strumble Head

Pen Caer

Dinas Island

Fishguard Bay

Pembrokeshire Coast Path

Nevern

213 △

Goodwick

Dinas

Newport ℹ A 487

Fishguard

★ Pentre Ifan

Ynys Deullyn

Abercastle

A 40

W. Cleddau

334 △

Presely Hills

536 △

Penclegyr

Porthgain

Letterston

347 △

B 4329

Llys-y-Frân Reservoir

Abereiddy

Solva

St David's Head

181 △

164 △

Wolf's Castle

Whitesands Bay

St David's ★★ ℹ

★ Scolton Museum and Country Park

St Justinians

Solva

Syfynwy

Porthclais

Newgale

Ramsey Island

Pembrokeshire Coast Path

Nolton

Rudbaxton

A 487

Llawhaden Castel

St Brides Bay

Haverfordwest ℹ

B 4341

A 40

Broad Haven

B 4076

Blackpool Mill

★ Skomer Island

Marloes Peninsula

St Brides

Johnston

Daugleddau

Picton Castle

B 4327

Broad Sound

Marloes Sands

Dale

Milford Haven

A 477

Upton Castle

A 4075

★ Skokholm Island

Neyland

Carew Castle ★

Thorn I.

Dale Peninsula

★ St Ann's Head

Angle

Pembroke Dock

Pembroke Castle ★★ ℹ

Rosslare

B 4320

Lamphey Bishop's Palace

Castlemartin

B 4319

Manorbier Castle

Linney Head

Bosherston

★ Stack Rocks

Stackpole Head

St Govan's Chapel ★

0 ——— 12 km
0 ——— 5 miles

78

Pembrokeshire is a peninsula divided by bays and by Milford Haven into further peninsulas projecting westward towards Ireland and the Atlantic. Together with the region's diverse geology, this makes for an

Michelin Atlas p 14 or Map 503
EFG 27-28-29
Tourist Information Centre – The Barbecue, Harbour Car Park, Saundersfoot,
SA69 9HE ☎ *01834 813 672;*
Fax 01834 813 673.

astonishing variety of coastal scenery. Great headlands of hard rock are separated by bays scooped out of softer materials by the action of the sea, sheltered sandy shores contrast with storm beaches piled high with pebbles, while rock stacks and offshore islands offer sanctuary to countless seabirds.

■ Historical notes

The area abounds in the dolmens, megaliths and promontory forts of prehistory. One of the finest burial chambers in Britain, **Pentre Ifan**, stands on the slopes of the **Presely Hills** (*Mynydd Preseli*), a mysterious, brooding upland in the northern, inland section of the Park (*see below*) which is considered to be the source of the bluestones from which Stonehenge was built.

Pembrokeshire is even more deeply suffused with the spirit of early Christianity, its wild shores settled by the monks and mystics of the Celtic Church who laid the spiritual foundations from which the great Cathedral of St David's later rose. Among many lesser examples, there are two of the three finest **Celtic crosses** in Wales at Carew and Nevern.

The Normans quickly consolidated their hold on this part of the country, a stepping stone to their later operations in Ireland, by building castles and settling the south of the area with so many English as well as Flemish immigrants that it has long been known as "Little England beyond Wales". A boundary known as the **Landsker** marked a military and later linguistic frontier between this southern "Englishry" and the "Welshry", the less fertile northern fastness into which the native Welsh unwillingly retreated. Church architecture still marks the difference between these cultural regions, the substantial southern churches having characteristic tall and fortified Pembrokeshire towers, the northern churches being of more modest construction, often with a small belfry rather than a tower.

Pembrokeshire Coast National Park – This is the smallest as well as the least typical of Great Brit-

Out and About

Puffin Shuttle – The Puffin Shuttle service, which helps to ease congestion in the Park by enabling visitors to leave their cars behind, operates every day in summer between St David's and Milford Haven.

Boat Trips – From Solva to Ramsey Island *(see also St David's)* by inflatable craft.

Coastal Footpath – This footpath runs the whole length of the Park from its southeastern boundary at Amroth to Poppit Sands near Cardigan in the north, a wonderful experience, if walked from end to end, but equally satisfying if enjoyed in shorter stretches.

Activities – Most kinds of seaside activities can be enjoyed in the Park, from surfing, sailing and water-skiing, to sea-angling, birdwatching, or simply sitting on the beach.

Beaches – On the south Coast at Amroth, Saundersfoot, Freshwater East, Barafundle Bay, Broad Haven, Bosherston, West Angle Bay *(see also Tenby)*; on the west coast at Neyland Marina; Gelliswick, Milford Haven; Dale; Marloes Sands; Martin's Haven; St Bride's Haven; Little Haven, Broad Haven and Nolton Haven *(see also St David's and Fishguard)*.

Caravan Parks – There are many caravan parks; their proliferation has been one of the Park planners' greatest problems.

Craft Centres – For woollen goods visit **The Woollen Mill** *(Middle Mill, Solva)*.

ain's National Parks, extending not over mountain or hill country but over the cliffs and beaches of one of the country's most spectacular and fascinating coastlines (180mi/ 290km).

Since its designation in 1952, the National Park's manifold natural attractions have drawn ever-increasing numbers of visitors. Most are holiday-makers, staying for a week or two; in spite of road improvements, Pembrokeshire is still a good distance from South Wales and England, so day trippers are relatively few.

The oil installations, which many thought would destroy the landscape of Milford Haven for ever, have now had 30 years to settle into the scene, and the movements of the supertankers in and out of the Haven have become an attraction in themselves.

Still controversial are the activities of the Army, which was testing its tanks on Castlemartin ranges long before the National Park was created. Gunfire may be disturbing but military occupation keeps out the pressures of intensive farming; uncontaminated by insecticides and herbicides, the ranges are now a refuge for all kinds of wildlife. ■

PORT TALBOT

Playing Vesuvius in the fanciful comparison of Swansea Bay with the Bay of Naples, the cooling towers, chimneys and smoky pall of Port Talbot dominate the eastern shore of this splendid coastal crescent with its backing of hills and mountains.

No traveller heading westward out of the Vale of Glamorgan can fail to become aware of Port Talbot. Squeezed into the narrow strip of land between the shore and abruptly rising hills, the main railway line and motorway are forced into intimate contact with the town. The steel-

Neath Port Talbot – Population 47 299
Michelin Atlas p 15 or Map 503 I 29

works stretch for nearly 5mi/8km, accompanied by a number of more recent industrial plants. The industrial picture is completed to the west by extensive chemical works, while the housing estates, in which most of Port Talbot's population live sprawl between the small town centre and **Aberavon Sands**, which are backed by a promenade. ■

OLD RADNOR

(Pencraig) Powys

Today Old Radnor, which was replaced in the 13C by the planned settlement of New Radnor, is hardly more than a hamlet but it has kept a parish church of unusual size and beauty.

Michelin Atlas pp 25 and 26 or Map 503 K 27

St Stephen's Church★ – The church stands in a round graveyard high up (840ft/256m) on the slopes of Old Radnor Hill with fine views northwestwards to Radnor Forest. The present 15C and early-16C building in Perpendicular style was preceded by a Norman structure which itself probably replaced an ancient Welsh foundation.

New Radnor – *3mi/5km west of Old Radnor.* Laid out in the mid 13C on a characteristic grid pattern, New Radnor was one of several planned towns in the Marches which failed to meet their founders' expectations. ■

RAGLAN CASTLE★

Monmouthshire

With Raglan... the long era of castle-building in Wales comes to a magnificent end" (John Hilling). The substantial ruins of this great late-medieval stronghold, crowning a rise above the modern Monmouth-Abergavenny road, exemplify the taste, wealth and sophistication of its 15C and later owners, concerned as much with

Michelin Atlas p 16 or Map 503 L 28

ostentation and luxury as with defence. Fine stonework, the remains of sumptuous decoration and the traces of what were some of the finest gardens in Britain evoke the expansive way of life lived by its early owners. ■

VALE OF RHEIDOL*

Ceredigion

Michelin Atlas p 24 or Map 503 I 26

The landscape in this valley was probably shaped by volcanic forces. The compressed silts which form the local rocks may have been heaved into their present position by ancient volcanoes but the falls and chasms are the result of the phenomenon known as river capture. Rheidol and Mynach, its tributary, originally flowed roughly southwards but a shorter stream, flowing westward to the coast, cut back into the course of the Rheidol in the uplands and "captured" their waters, so that the Rheidol now describes a dramatic right-angled bend and falls precipitously into the bed of its new partner.

Vale of Rheidol Railway★★ *(See town plan of Aberystwyth p 27–* **AB X**). No standard-gauge track could possibly have performed the contortions necessary to adapt the line to the steep sides of the glaciated valley and to overcome the change in level (480ft/146m) in the final stretch (4mi/6km) between Aberffrwd and Devil's Bridge. This section is a true mountain railway; locomotives N° 7 *Owain Glyndwr* or N° 9 *Prince of Wales* have to work hard to beat gradients of up to 1 in 48. In places the train runs along a rocky ledge, elsewhere tunnelling through a green vault of ferns, birch and ancient oakwood, with glimpses of the Vale far below, before arriving at the Devil's Bridge terminus.

Devil's Bridge Waterfalls★ – The waterfalls on the River Mynach plunging into the deep wooded chasm at the head of the Vale of Rheidol attracted Romantic tourists like Wordsworth, who came here in 1824.

The first bridge across the gully carved out by the Mynach may have been built by the monks of Strata Florida Abbey.

Above the simple stone arch of this medieval bridge are two successors, one dating from about 1708 and the other an iron structure built at the beginning of the 20C, when the Vale of Rheidol Railway began to bring large numbers of visitors to what had become one of the most famous sights in Wales.

The waterfalls in their setting of moss-grown rock and wonderful oak woodland are fenced off and must be approached through turnstiles. ∎

ST DAVID'S ★★

On its far western peninsula, this tiniest of British cities exerts the same pull on today's visitors as it did on the medieval pilgrims making their way to the shrine of St David, the patron saint of Wales.

Dewi Sant – Tradition has it that St David (AD c 462-520) was born during a thunderstorm on the windswept clifftop where a chapel was subsequently dedicated to his mother, St Non *(see below)*. The monastery he founded was located a little further inland, in the marshy valley through which the little River Alun makes its way to the sea, and it is here, on a drier shelf of land just above the stream, that today's superb cathedral stands.

The wildness and remoteness of the spot suited the demands of monastic life. David himself practised an asceticism even more strict than that of his monks, drenching himself in cold water to still the urgings of the flesh, hence his name "David the Waterman", although it may refer

(Tyddewi) Pembrokeshire – Population 1 959 Michelin Atlas p 14 or Map 503 E 28 Tourist Information Centre – National Park Visitor Centre, The Grove, St David's SA62 6NW ☎ 01437 720 392; Fax 01437 720 099.

to his refusal to touch alcohol. His monastery may have enjoyed the seclusion of its inland valley site but its peninsula setting put it in contact with the ancient seaways linking Britain, the Continent and Ireland, making it accessible to the pilgrims who thronged to what became the saint's shrine. This openness to the ocean also made the monastery vulnerable to attack from less benign seafarers; after a series of Viking raids in the 10C and 11C, the site was abandoned.

© Wales Tourist Board

■ Cathedral close

The pastoral setting of Palace and Cathedral in their hollow, with farmland beyond, and within the protection of the close wall, is uniquely evocative of the religious life of the Middle Ages, even though none of the clergy residences are older than the 18C. The presence of orchards and grazing land within the precinct can easily be imagined, while the little tower built at the point where the Alun leaves the close probably controlled the flow of water to adjacent fishponds.

St David's Cathedral★★ – The unique appeal of the finest church in Wales is due partly to the way in which it suddenly reveals itself to the visitor. Seen from Tower Gate (Porth y Tŵr) which forms the entrance to the precinct from the city, the great building of finely textured and coloured stone seems to fill the valley, its centrepiece the tall tower which helps to draw the contribution of different building periods into a harmonious whole.

Bishop's Palace★ – The palace of the Bishops of St David's lies on the far bank of the Alun, proclaiming, even in ruin, the power, wealth and taste of these ecclesiastical magnates. ■

SWANSEA*

A city of strong and varied personality, Swansea is the un-rivalled capital of southwestern Wales, with a commercial centre rebuilt after war-time bombing, a revitalised maritime quarter, a university and a dramatic setting on the splendid sweep of its great bay.

The uplands of central Wales come rolling almost to the waterfront, the city has its own seaside resort of The Mumbles, and to the west are the cliffs, beaches and unspoilt countryside of the Gower Peninsula, Britain's first officially designated Area of Outstanding Natural Beauty (AONB).

Cultural life is at least as vibrant as that of the capital, Cardiff. Once a focal point of the Industrial Revolution, the city has cleared away the dereliction left by centuries of reckless industrial development and is proud of its heritage of parks, gardens and other green spaces.

Swansea's more salubrious suburbs extend westwards. They include Edwardian Uplands, where **Dylan Thomas** was born and passed his early years in what he called "this lovely, ugly town", often musing in Cwmdonkin Park where there is a memorial to him.

(Abertawe) Swansea – Population 181 906
Michelin Atlas p 15 or Map 503 I 29
Tourist Information Centres – Plymouth Street, Swansea SA1 3QG
☎ *01792 468 321;*
Fax 01792 464 602;
swantrsm@cableol.co.uk
Oystermouth Square, Mumbles SA3 4DQ ☎ *01792 361 302;*
Fax 01792 363 392.

■ Maritime quarter* (B)

A succession of docks was built throughout the 19C to cater for what seemed like an ever-expanding influx of shipping, bringing in ores from Cornwall and beyond and taking out the coal from the 200 or so pits around the city. Today, the commercial docks, including the car ferry to Cork, are all to the east of the Tawe, now controlled by a **new barrage (C)** and lock. On the far bank, close to the city centre, the South Dock was built in 1859, occupying the once-fashionable area known as the Burrows and putting paid to Swansea's aspirations as a resort. The wheel has now come full-circle; closed in 1969, the dock

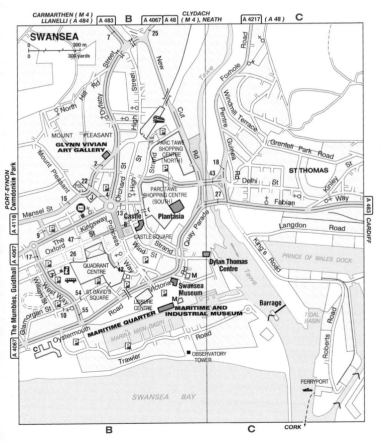

Out and About

Entertainment – The lively **cultural life** of Swansea includes regular concerts by international orchestras and soloists in the **Brangwyn Hall** (Box Office ☎ 01792 302 489), opera and ballet and touring productions in the **Grand Theatre** (Box Office ☎ 01792 475 715), a variety of productions in the smaller theatres – **Dylan Thomas Theatre** (☎ 01792 473 238), the **Taliesin Theatre** (Box Office ☎ 01792 296 883) and the **Cwmtawe Theatre** (Box Office ☎ 01792 830 111) and **Penyrheol Theatre** (Box Office ☎ 01792 897 039).

Festivals – The most popular of the local festivals are the **Swansea Summer Show** (August), **Swansea Festival of Music** (Autumn), the **Margam Festival** (July-August) and the **Llanelli Festival** (September-October), the **Gower Festival** of small concerts in the churches of the area (July); except in summer visitors may attend the rehearsals of the famous **Male voice choirs**.

Craftwork – The **Lovespoon Gallery** *(Mumbles Road, Oystermouth)* offers a wide range of lovespoons in different designs and types of wood, also varying sizes and prices. For woollen goods visit the **Maritime and Industrial Museum** *(see below)* and see the machinery from the Neath **Abbey Woollen Mill** in action.

Indoor Activities – The Swansea Leisure Centre provides for many such – swimming (water slide and diving tank), roller skating, squash, Badminton, trampoline, volleyball, martial arts, table tennis, bowling, sauna, steam room, sunbeds.

Outdoor Activities – These make the most of the natural elements – sea and wind – canoeing, sailing, surfing (Bay Caswell and Langland Bay or Llangennith for the Atlantic rollers), windsurfing (Oxwich, Port Eynon), waterskiing (Swansea Bay, Oxwich Bay), hang-gliding and parascending (Rhossili Bay). Good beach at Swansea Marina.

has been saved from dereliction and transformed into the sparkling centrepiece of what the city proudly calls its Maritime Quarter, with an array of new housing, a marina for 600 boats, restaurants, a theatre, a gallery, a luxury hotel and a fine museum. The whole area has been enriched with public art, which ranges from an engaging statue of **Dylan Thomas** on the quayside to quizzical sculptures on a maritime theme along the new promenade facing Swansea Bay.

Maritime and Industrial Museum★ (B) – Housed in the former Coast Lines warehouse, this is an important museum, a stimulating starting point for any appreciation of Swansea and its setting. The emphasis is on the city's long-standing connection with the sea, on industry and on transport.

Dylan Thomas Centre (BC) – *Somerset Place*. The former Guildhall, a colonnaded Georgian building overlooking the marina, has been transformed into the **National Literature Centre for Wales**, which houses a theatre, exhibition galleries and a meeting room for writers and artists. A permanent, though changing, exhibition explores the life and friendships of **Dylan Thomas** through photographs, letters and film. New and second-hand works are on sale in the bookshop-cum-café.

■ City centre

Swansea's commercial heart is crammed into the narrow strip of land between the shoreline and the abruptly rising slopes just to the north, now covered with suburban housing.

The centre, severely battered by the enemy bombing in 1941, makes few claims to obvious historical or architectural interest but pulses with vigorous life, especially around the famous covered Market with its fabulous range of fresh foods. The modern retail centres of The Quadrant and St David's pick up the theme of crowded shopping under cover. Close by is the Grand Theatre, still with its auditorium of 1897.

Princess Way and Kingsway reflect post-war planners' none-too-successful attempts to dignify the city centre with grandiose boulevards but Castle Square is currently being expensively restyled and landscaped to make it a more fitting focal point.

Glynn Vivian Art Gallery★ (B) – This airy yet intimate gallery was opened in 1911 to house the art collections donated to the city by Glynn Vivian (1835-1910), a member of the wealthy dynasty who had made Swansea the copper capital of the world. The collections reflect not only this eccentric younger son's extensive travels in Europe, but also the pre-eminence of the famous Swansea (later Cambrian) Pottery in the late 18C-early 19C.

Swansea Marina

© Wales Tourist Board

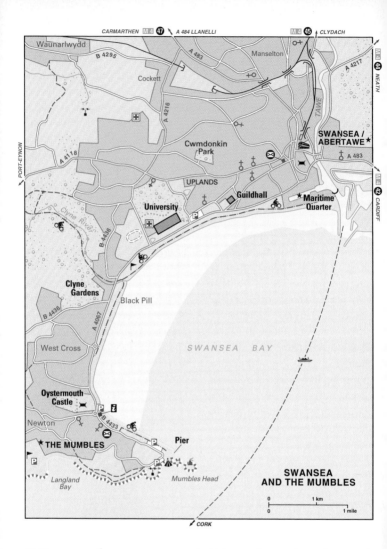

Waunarlwydd

B 4295

Cockett

A 493

Manselton

A 4217

TAWE

M4 44 NEATH

PORT-EYNON

A 4118

Cwmdonkin
Park

SWANSEA /
ABERTAWE ★

A 483

M4 42 CARDIFF

Clyne River

UPLANDS

Guildhall

★ Maritime
Quarter

University

B 4436

P

Clyne
Gardens

Black Pill

B 4436

A 4067

West Cross

SWANSEA BAY

Oystermouth
Castle

P i

Newton

B 4433

THE MUMBLES

Pier

P

P

P

Langland
Bay

Mumbles Head

SWANSEA
AND THE MUMBLES

0   1 km

0   1 mile

CORK

■ Swansea bay

To the west of the mouth of the Tawe, the splendid shoreline curves round in a tightening crescent that ends in the rock islands of Mumbles Head and is accompanied for its entire length by a chain of parks and other green spaces. The main highway, almost always busy with traffic, parallels a cycleway laid out along the promenade which replaced the much-mourned **Mumbles Railway**. This famous and fascinating line, claimed to have been the first passenger railway in the world, extended from its dockside station all along the seafront to Mumbles Pier and seemed for many years an irreplaceable part of city life. It was built in 1804 and carried passengers from 1807 onwards until, underfunded and with outworn rolling stock, it was closed in 1960.

At weekends or on fine evenings the exodus from the city intensifies as the population flocks westward for the fresher air of the Mumbles or of the Gower Peninsula just beyond. The prospect of sea, city and hills has sometimes been compared to the Bay of Naples, a hyperbole forgivable on a summer evening when the Bristol Channel tides have covered the extensive mudflats. A modern County Hall has taken advantage of the view, and those able to afford it have always resided in this part of the city, well to windward of the source of their wealth, the pollution-producing enterprises lining the Tawe to the east of the city.

The Mumbles★ – Mumbles has a multiple personality. Its 13C castle has looked down on oystermen, mansion-dwellers and sedate Victorian holidaymakers as well as today's yachtsmen and other watersports enthusiasts. The difficult approach to Swansea Bay is guarded both by the lighthouse and by the famous Mumbles lifeboat.

The Mumbles has become the city's favourite suburb, both for commuting residents and for the weekend revellers who throng the pubs and restaurants crowded along the waterfront road. Bathers nowadays prefer the smaller bays at Langland and Caswell to the west of Mumbles Head. ■

TINTERN ABBEY★★

Monmouthshire

The Cistercians came to this remote and lovely location amid the woods of the winding Wye in 1131, and the picturesque ruins of their great abbey still stand, a magnet for visitors ever since the first tourists floated down the river in search of sublime and romantic scenery in the late 18C.

Its roof gone, its glass smashed, its walls obliterated by ivy, the abbey church nevertheless remains essentially intact and, although the greater part of its extensive outbuildings have been reduced to stubs of walls, Tintern still conveys a powerful impression of the architectural splendour which accompanied the severities of monastic life.

Norman Foundation – Tintern was the first Cistercian abbey to be established in Wales, a daughter house of the abbey at L'Aumone in Normandy, whose monks were invited here by Walter Fitz Richard de Clare of Chepstow Castle *(see p 58)*. The lords of Chepstow were to continue as benefactors of the abbey, the greatest of them being Roger Bigod III who was responsible for the lavish rebuilding of the abbey church in the late 13C. By the time of the Dissolution, Tin-

Michelin Atlas p 16 or Map 503 L 28

tern was the wealthiest abbey in Wales, a complex of buildings extending over much of the narrow strip of flat land between the river and the steep wooded slopes.

Romantic Tintern – In the mid 18C the abbey ruins were taken in hand by the Duke of Beaufort, who tidied and turfed the interior, thus making it ready for the tourists who were soon to arrive.

Among the first was the Revd William Gilpin, one of the foremost promoters of "Picturesque" sensibility, who, in his *Observations on the River Wye* (1782), suggested that the ruins might benefit from the judicious use of a mallet to knock them into even more attractively irregular shape. Equipped with his book, parties of visitors would descend the river from Ross to Chepstow in boats provided by local innkeepers, who by special arrangement would also provide a torchlight tour of the abbey ruins by night.

The elegiac atmosphere sought by such visitors was captured by **JMW Turner** (1755-1851) who made a number of studies of the ruins in the course of the 1790s. Tintern occupied a special place in the heart of **William Wordsworth** (1770-1850), who came here twice, in 1793 and again in 1798, composing his famous *Lines Written a Few Miles above Tintern Abbey* which recall:

> ... *these steep and lofty cliffs,*
> *Which on a wild secluded scene*
> *impress*
> *Thoughts of more deep seclusion....*

Abbey Ruins – Souvenir shops and car and coach parks attest to Tintern's longstanding popularity. Entry is via discreetly-designed modern buildings flanking the riverside car park, and most visitors will be drawn first to the majestic **abbey church,** built, unusually, to the south of the cloister and its surrounding buildings. With its high walls crowned by the four great gables of nave, transepts and sanctuary, this is the structure raised by the munificence of Roger Bigod between 1269 and 1301 to replace the far more modest 12C Norman church whose outline is marked on the floor of the nave.

All the screens and subdivisions which reflected the complexities of monastic ritual have long since disappeared, and the eye is led directly to the far end of the building, where the **east window (1)**, bare of all tracery and with but a single central mullion, links the abbey with its gloriously wooded setting. Columns, shafts and pointed arches in Decorated style still evoke something of the confidence and expansiveness of the late 13C, but it is the great, seven-light **west**

window (2) which is the most splendid surviving single feature. In the presbytery, massive upturned roof bosses are reminders of the weight and substance of the stone vaults which disappeared at the Dissolution.

Bigod's late-13C rebuilding of the abbey church had been preceded earlier in the century by reconstruction of the accommodation around the **cloisters.**

Along the north side are substantial remains of the monks' dining hall, flanked by **kitchen** to the west and **warming house** to the east. Still partly vaulted, this last structure housed the abbey's only permanent winter fire, where monks might recover from the chilling effects of protracted worship in otherwise stone-cold surroundings.

The western range of the cloister contained the quarters of the lay brothers; to the east are the remains of the chapter-house, nov-ices' lodging and monks' dormitory. The foundations of the latrine block are visible, once flushed by the drain which runs roughly west-east across the whole site; its alignment may have forced the reversal of the traditional Cistercian siting of church to the north and cloister to the south, to maximise natural light and warmth.

The abbey precinct (27 acres/11ha) extended over an area larger than that of most medieval Welsh towns. To the east of the main cloister, a secondary cloister developed, dominated by the infirmary and by the abbot's quarters (4), both of which were added to and improved in the course of the 14C and 15C. To the west of the complex, there are foundations of the guest house, the arch of the watergate leading to the river; the gatehouse chapel has been converted into a house and parts of the precinctual wall now enclose private gardens. ■

TREDEGAR HOUSE ★★

Newport

Tredegar is one of the grandest houses of the post-Civil War period in the whole of England and Wales. It was the residence of the enormously-rich **Morgan** family until death duties reduced their inheritance.

After 20 years of attrition caused by its use as a school, it passed into public ownership and is now the

Michelin Atlas p 16 or Map 503 K 29

jewel in Newport's civic crown. As the process of sensitive restoration continues, Tredegar has recovered its spirit, and is now as fascinating inside as out. Its well-tree'd grounds have become a popular country park. ■

MUSEUM OF WELSH LIFE★★★

Cardiff

In 1947 the Tudor mansion known as St Fagans Castle and some of its grounds (100 acres/42ha) were made available to the nation by the Earl of Plymouth. An important open-air museum of vernacular buildings has been established on the site and is now one of the country's most visited tourist attractions.

The museum is devoted to the serious study and conservation of Welsh folk culture and aims to show how Welsh people lived and worked from the 16C-17C onwards. At its heart is the array of more than 30 traditional structures from all parts of Wales, rescued from demolition and re-erected here.

The Castle itself serves as a complementary exhibit, a reminder of the social and economic interdependence of gentry and common people. Great efforts have gone into giving the museum a lived-in atmosphere; the trades and crafts once practised in many of the buildings are still carried on in them; traditional breeds of farm animal roam the hedged or fenced enclosures dividing up the parkland, and events and festivals are held throughout the year.

Michelin Atlas p 16 or Map 503 K 29 – 5mi/8km west of Cardiff in St Fagans

■ Tour

Galleries – The museum presents a somewhat intimidating face to the outside world, in the shape of the long and low modern edifice housing service facilities and galleries. The galleries themselves are spacious and allow the wealth of objects on display to be appreciated fully.

The array of implements in the **Agriculture Gallery** helps trace the development of farming techniques in a land which environmental conditions often made difficult to work and remind the visitor of the importance of livestock farming in a mountainous country.

The **Costume Gallery** is dimly lit in order to preserve the fragile evidence of how the Welsh have dressed since the beginning of the 18C.

The **Gallery of Material Culture** has an extraordinary accumulation of instruments and artefacts relating to all aspects of daily life, from tools, toys, games, guns and swords, to musical instruments, kitchen implements, Welsh dressers and love spoons.

Open-air Section – The museum's collection of old buildings is still growing, and space is available for further structures. The buildings are dispersed over the extensive site, some arranged in interesting groupings, others related to their own carefully devised and authentic-seeming context of garden, yard or forecourt. The materials of walls and roofs reflect the diversity of Welsh landscapes; coarse stonework is exposed to magnificently bold effect in **Y Garreg Fawr** farmhouse (1544) but is often rendered, as are the walls of **Nantwallter Cottage** (1770), made of clom, a form of cob composed of clay, gravel and straw. The 17C black-and-white **Abernodwydd farmhouse** from Powys tells of close links with English traditions of timber construction. Furnishings have been chosen to evoke a particular period, not always that of the time when the building was first erected.

The primary theme is that of farming, with fascinating examples of how accommodation for both people and animals has evolved since all lived together in the **Hendre'r-ywydd Uchaf longhouse** (1508), from Llangynhafal

in northeast Wales, to the **Llwyn-yr-Eos farmstead** (1820), still on its original site on the banks of the River Ely and eloquent testimony to the rationality and relative comfort of Georgian times. Other farmhouses include **Kennixton** (early 17C) from the Gower peninsula, painted red to discourage evil spirits, and there are labourers' cottages, barns and a corbelled drystone pigsty resembling the *trulli* of southern Italy. There are barns and a hayshed, the **Melin Bompren cornmill** (working) and, more unusually, a little mill which reduced the prickly sprigs of gorse to palatable horse fodder.

Examples of enterprises serving the rural economy include a **sawmill**, a **woollen mill**, a **tannery** and a working **bakery**, while among community buildings are an 18C **Unitarian chapel**, a **Victorian school**, a tiny **post office**, the well-stocked **Gwalia Stores**, and, the largest edifice on site, the **Oakdale Workmen's Institute** (1916), the equivalent of a modern leisure centre. A 17C thatched circular **cockpit** from the *Hawk and Buckle Inn* in Denbigh recalls the crueller pleasures of an earlier age.

A **tollhouse** is furnished in the style of 1843, a year which saw the destruction of many tollgates by the Rebecca Rioters. ∎

PRACTICAL INFORMATION

■ Planning a trip ■

Seasons – Summer is the best time for visiting Wales and enjoying its natural attractions on the coast or in the mountains. Spring and autumn are good seasons for visiting parks and gardens when the flowers are in bloom or the leaves are turning colour. The tourist season, when the main festivals are held, runs from Easter to October. At any time of year there is the possibility of rain, owing to the mountains and the prevailing westerly wind; in winter there may be snow, especially on the high ground.

The **Wales Tourist Board** provides assistance in planning a trip to Wales and an excellent range of brochures and maps.

Wales Tourist Board, Brunel House, 2 Fitzalan Road, Cardiff CF24 0UY; ☎ 029 2047 5226 (brochures); ☎ 029 2049 9909 (switchboard); Fax 029 2047 5345; info@tourism.wales.gov.uk; www.visitwales.com

Mid-Wales Tourism: The Station, Machynlleth SY20 8TG; ☎ 0800 273 7 47 (freephone); ☎ 01654 702 653; Fax 01654 703 235; mwt@mid-wales-tourism.org.uk; www.mid-wales-tourism.org.uk

Tourism South and West Wales: Charter Court, Enterprise Park, Swansea SA7 9DB; ☎ 01792 781 212; Fax 01792 781 300; croeso@tsww.com; www.tsww.org.uk

Wales Information Bureau, British Visitor Centre, 1 Lower Regent Street, London SW1 4XT; ☎ 020 8846 9000 (British Tourist Authority); 020 7808 3838 (Enquiries about Wales).

There are **Tourist Information Centres** in all parts of the country with information on sightseeing, accommodation, places to eat, transport, entertainment, sports and local events. They are usually well signed but some are open only during the summer season; addresses and telephone numbers are given in each chapter.

Special Needs

Many of the sights described in this guide are accessible to disabled people.

The Wales Tourist Board issues a pamphlet *Discovering Accessible Wales* which gives advice for disabled people on holiday in Wales.

Organisations such as the British Tourist Authority, National Trust and the Department of Transport publish booklets for the disabled.

The *Michelin Red Guide Great Britain and Ireland* indicates hotels with facilities suitable for disabled people; it is advisable to book in advance.

■ Getting there ■

By Air – Cardiff-Wales airport (12mi/19km west of Cardiff city centre) at Rhoose in the Vale of Glamorgan has daily scheduled flights to a number of cities in the UK, Ireland and continental Europe with world-wide connections via Manchester and Amsterdam. The international airports at Manchester and Birmingham are accessible from many parts of Wales and London Heathrow is 140mi/225km from Cardiff via the M4 motorway.

Information, brochures and timetables are available from the airlines and from travel agents. Many airlines organise fly-drive facilities.

Three major airports serve passengers travelling to Wales; two are just over the border in England; Cardiff and Birmingham offer long-term parking

– Cardiff Airport ☎ 01446 711 111;

– Birmingham International Airport ☎ 0121 767 5511;

– Manchester Airport ☎ 0161 489 3000;

– Fairwood Airport near Swansea (a smaller airport for light aircraft) ☎ 01792 468 321 (Swansea TIC).

By Rail – Fast rail services link major towns in South and North Wales with London and other English cities and also connect with ferry services to and from Fishguard and Holyhead.

By Bus and Coach – A network of express coach services run by a number of operators covers most of Wales. North and South Wales are linked by the TrawsCambria line between Cardiff, Aberystwyth and Bangor. Details available from Tourist Information Centres and local bus stations. Connections to the rest of Great Britain are run by National Express.

National Express, Birmingham; ☎ 08705 808 080 (National call centre); ☎ 0121 625 1122; Fax 0121 456 1397 (Head Office); www.gobycoach.com

■ Motoring ■

South Wales is linked to the national motorway network by the M4 motorway while a highway of near-motorway standard, the North Wales Expressway, connects the towns and resorts of the north coast to the north of England. Main roads generally are well engineered and relatively uncrowded, though the nature of the country imposes many bends and steep gradients. Special care needs to be taken on minor roads, especially in mountainous areas and in other places where grazing animals may be a hazard.

Route Planning – Wales is covered by the *Michelin Road Atlas of Great Britain and Ireland* (scale 1:300 000) and by *Michelin Map 503* (scale: 1:400 000). In addition to the usual detailed road information they show tourist features such as beaches and bathing areas, swimming pools, golf courses, racecourses, scenic routes, tourist sights, country parks etc. These publications are an essential complement to the annual *Michelin Red Guide Great Britain and Ireland*, which offers an up-to-date selection of hotels and restaurants.

Car Rental – There are car rental agencies at Cardiff-Wales airport, at railway stations and in larger towns and resorts throughout Wales.

■ Places to stay ■

It is advisable to book well in advance for the holiday season.

Booking service – Most Tourist Information Centres will arrange accommodation for a small fee. Room prices, even for a double room, may be quoted per person.

Publications – Most Tourist Information Centres provide, free of charge, an information booklet listing hotels, bed and breakfast and other accommodation in their area. The **Wales Tourist Board** *(see p 102)* publishes a number of magazines (free of charge) which provide a selection of hotels, guesthouses, farmhouse accommodation, self-catering properties and caravan parks:

Wales Countryside Holidays and *Wales Farm Holidays.*

Hotels – There is a full range of hotel accommodation from the most expensive and formal to smaller and more modest establishments. Accommodation guides are available from Tourist Information Centres. See below for some suggestions.

The two rates quoted for each establishment refer to the nightly rate of a single or double room. Breakfast may not always be included in the price. Some restaurants listed below may also have rooms.

ABERGAVENNY
Pantrhiwgoch, Brecon Rd, Llanwenarth, NP8 1EP, ☎ (01873) 810550; info@pantrhiwgoch.co.uk – £63-£73. Part 16C inn; perches on banks of river Usk, famed for salmon, trout fishing. Most bedrooms have balconies from which to enjoy panoramas of Blorenge Mountain and Usk Valley. Tall-windowed dining room with fine valley views and home-made food.

ABERYSTWYTH
Conrah Country House, Chancery (Rhydgaled), SY23 4DF, ☎ (01970) 617941; enquiries@conrah.co.uk – £87-£150. Part 18C mansion, elegant inside and out. Lovely grounds, kitchen garden, pleasant views. Airy country house rooms include three very smart new ones in converted outbuildings. Scenic vistas greet restaurant diners.

BONVILSTON
The Great Barn, Lillypot, CF5 6TR, ☎ (01446) 781010; nina@greatbarn.com – £40-£65. Converted corn barn in Vale of Glamorgan. Personally run in simple style of a country home. Pine and white furniture in rooms; some pleasant antiques. Great view at breakfast.

BRIDGEND
Travelodge, Pencoed, CF3 5HU, ☎ (08700) 850950 – £80. Maintains the group's reputation for affordable accommodation and simple contemporary styling. Sofa beds and convenient work surfaces are useful features.

CAERSWS

Lower Ffrydd, SY17 5QS, ☎ (01686) 688269; loffrydd@dircon.co.uk – £30-£50. Richly characterful 16C farmhouse on working farm. Fine views of rolling mid-Wales countryside. Two oak-beamed drawing rooms, one with huge panoramic window. Stylish rooms. Elegant, communal breakfast room with inglenook fireplace and fine views.

Cefn-Gwyn Farm, Trefeglwys, SY17 5RF, ☎ (01686) 430648; cefngwyn@btconnect.com – £28-£50. Well cared for, whitewashed farmhouse on working farm. Views over surrounding countryside. Large, inviting conservatory lounge. Rooms furnished to good standard. Friendly owners take pride in using fresh regional produce in simple but sustaining evening meals.

CARDIFF

Express by Holiday Inn, Longueil Close, Atlantic Wharf, CF10 4EE, ☎ (029) 2044 9000; silke@firstinn.co.uk – £67. Ideal for both corporate and leisure travellers and even meetings can be held here. Overlooking the waterfront and within the up-and-coming Bay area. Well-equipped rooms.

Travelodge, 65-67 St Marys St, Imperial Gate, CF10 1FA, ☎ (08700) 850950 – £80. Functional lodge accommodation, offering spacious and clean bedrooms, all with sofa beds. Handy for the Millennium Stadium and the shopping arcades.

Townhouse, 70 Cathedral Rd, CF11 9LL, ☎ (029) 2023 9399; thetownhouse@msn.com – £43-£73. Carefully restored Victorian house with Gothic features. Welcoming service by owners. Light and airy bedrooms have some thoughtful touches and are well-appointed.

CARDIGAN

Gwbert, Gwbert on Sea, SA43 1PP, ☎ (01239) 612638; gwbert@enterprise.net – £45-£119. Traditional seaside hotel on banks of Teifi with inspiring views of Cardigan Bay. Bright pastel public areas and smart bar. Well-kept rooms with co-ordinated fabrics. Pink washed dining room with panoramic views of Pembroke National Park coastline.

CRICKHOWELL

Bear, High St, NP8 1BW, ☎ (01873) 810408; bearhotel@aol.com – £55-£135. Imposing, part 15C former coaching inn with maze of public areas. Bustling bar and lounges. Good conference facilities. Plush, spacious bedrooms with modern furnishings.

HAVERFORDWEST

Wilton House, 6 Quay St, SA61 1BG, ☎ (01437) 760033; office@wiltonhousehotel.co.uk – £40-£65. Georgian house conveniently located in the centre of town near shops and craft workshops. Bedrooms, commensurate with the age of the building, are large with high ceilings. The restaurant has something of an old-fashioned atmosphere and ambience.

HAY-ON-WYE
Old Post Office, Llanigon, HR3 5QA, ☎ (01497) 820008; – £28-£56. Dating from 17C, a converted inn. Near the «book town» of Hay-on-Wye. Smart modern ambience blends with characterful charm. Pine furnished rooms with polished floors.

HENSOL
Llanerch Vineyard, CF72 8GG, ☎ (01443) 225877; enquiries@llanerch-vineyard.co.uk – £50-£69. Rurally set, fully functioning vineyard in woodland with 20 acres of vines. The modern breakfast area is furnished with Welsh art. Immaculate, state of the art bedrooms.

KNIGHTON
Milebrook House, Ludlow Rd, Milebrook, LD7 1LT, ☎ (01547) 528632; hotel@milebrook.kc3ltd.co.uk – £58-£96. Located in the Teme Valley; good for exploring the Welsh Marches. Possesses a fine, formal garden well stocked with exotic plants. Rooms are large and pleasingly decorated. The kitchen garden provides most of the vegetables which appear in the restaurant.

LAKE VYRNWY
Lake Vyrnwy, SY10 0LY, ☎ (01691) 870692; res@lakevyrnwy.com – £90-£190. Victorian country house built from locally quarried stone overlooking the lake; an RSPB sanctuary and sporting estate, ideal for game enthusiasts. Rooms have timeless chic. Spectacular lakeside views from the restaurant are matched by accomplished cooking.

LLANDRINDOD WELLS
Acorn Court Country House, Chapel Rd, Howey, LD1 5PB, ☎ (01597) 823543; info@acorncourt.co.uk – £30-£60. Chalet-style house in lovely countryside; guests can fish in the lake. Bedrooms are large with many extra touches: hairdryers, stationery, soft toys-homely and welcoming.

Lasswade Country House, Station Rd, LD5 4RW, ☎ (01591) 610515; r.stevens@messages.co.uk – £55-£75. Smartly refurbished Edwardian country house, with fine views of mid-Wales countryside. Charming breakfast conservatory; cosy lounge. Bright, well-kept bedrooms. Proudly pro-organic meals the order of the day.

LLANTWIT MAJOR
West House Country, West St, CF61 1SP, ☎ (01446) 792406; enq@westhouse-hotel.co.uk – £58-£68. 16C hotel in Vale of Glamorgan. After cliff top walks, relax in beautiful, coir carpeted conservatory for afternoon tea. Rooms vary in size and style; all are immaculate. Heritage restaurant is decorated in a cottage style with mahogany chairs.

MONTGOMERY
Little Brompton Farm, SY15 6HY, ☎ (01686) 668371; gaynor.brompton@virgin.net – £30-£50. Part 17C ivy-clad cottage on a working farm, run by an friendly couple. En suite rooms in traditional fabrics. Cosy beamed lounge with inglenook fireplace. Hearty breakfast.

Garthmyl Hall, Garthmyl, SY15 6RS, ☎ (01686) 640550; – £50-£110. Fine part Georgian manor; a stylish, clean-lined reworking of classic interiors adds an accomplished modern touch. Bright rooms, smaller at the rear. 19C landscaped gardens.

NEWPORT

Cnapan, East St, SA42 0SY, ☎ (01239) 820575; cnapan@online-holidays.net – £42-£68. Pine-fitted bedrooms with floral fabrics and individual character in a genuinely friendly guest house, family run for over 15 years. Homely lounge has a wood-burning stove. Lace-covered tables and family photographs set the tone in the traditional dining room.

The Inn at The Elm Tree, St Brides Wentlooge, NP10 8SQ, ☎ (01633) 680225; inn@the-elm-tree.co.uk – £80-£120. Converted 19C barn; pristine, pine-furnished rooms in bright fabrics thoughtfully supplied with 21C mod cons. Unfussy lounge bar, its wicker armchairs padded with cushions. Immaculately set dining room; wide-ranging, Welsh-based dishes.

PORTH

Heritage Park, Coed Cae Rd, Trehafod, CF37 2NP, ☎ (01443) 687057; heritageparkhotel@talk21.com – £70-£88. Brick-built hotel in Rhondda Valley, adjacent to Heritage Park Centre; Museum of Mining close by. Countryside location, yet not far from Cardiff. Co-ordinated, modern rooms. Loft dining with verandah or conservatory options.

PORTHCAWL

Atlantic, West Drive, CF36 3LT, ☎ (01656) 785011; enquiries@atlantichotelporthcawl.co.uk – £59-£90. Midway between Cardiff and Swansea is this harbour side hotel offering traditional comfort and style and personal service. Simple bedrooms are spotlessly kept. The restaurant has a classic, traditional air with mahogany and burgundy décor.

RAGLAN

Travelodge, NP5 4BG, ☎ (08700) 850950 – £80. Conveniently positioned lodge hotel, close to famous castle. Economical, modern bedrooms, uniformly arranged and fitted with broad worktops and sofa beds.

ST DAVIDS

Warpool Court, SA62 6BN, ☎ (01437) 720300; warpool@enterprise.net – £99-£198. Over 3000 hand-painted tiles of Celtic or heraldic design decorate the interior of this 19C house. Modern bedrooms, some with views over neat lawned gardens to the sea. Classic menus served at simply set, dark wood tables.

SWANSEA

Morgans, Somerset Pl, SA1 1RR, ☎ (01792) 484848; info@morganshotel.co.uk – £100-£250. Recently converted hotel near docks. Contemporary feel: neutral colours, leather sofas. Splendid original features include soaring cupola. Very stylish rooms.

Beaumont, 72-73 Walter Rd, SA1 4QA, ☎ (01792) 643956; info@ beaumonthotel.co.uk – £60-£90. Traditional in spirit, a welcoming, family run, town house hotel in the western suburbs. Simple bedrooms-a few with sunken baths-combine modern and period furniture. Conservatory restaurant set in pink and white.

Norton House, 17 Norton Rd, The Mumbles, SA3 5TQ, ☎ (01792) 404891; n ortonhouse@btconnect.com – £73-£103. Georgian former master mariner's house, run with personable ease by a husband and wife team. Tidy rooms in traditional fabrics and furnishings-some have four-poster beds. Elegant, classically proportioned dining room, offset by French etched glassware.

Hillcrest House, 1 Higher Lane, The Mumbles, SA3 4NS, ☎ (01792) 363700; stay@hillcresthousehotel.com – £65-£95. Friendly and privately run; softly lit lounge with inviting sofas and armchairs; bright bedrooms, each with a subtle national emblem like thistles or Canadian maple leaves. Prints and tall wine racks adorn dining room.

Fairyhill, Reynoldston, Llanrhidian, SA3 1BS, ☎ (01792) 390139; postbox@fairyhill.net – £120-£190. Georgian country house in extensive parkland and gardens. Cosy lounge with fireside chairs. Individually furnished bedrooms with CD player and music from the library. Gower produce dominates seasonal menus.

TENBY
Broadmead, Heywood Lane, SA70 8DA, ☎ (01834) 842641; – £34-£68. Privately owned country house hotel. Traditionally styled public rooms include conservatory overlooking gardens. Individually decorated rooms with modern amenities. Dining room in the traditional style common to the other parts of the house.

TENBY
Penally Abbey, Penally (Penalun), SA70 7PY, ☎ (01834) 843033; penally.abbe y@btinternet.com – £126-£150. Gothic style, stone built house with attractive views of Carmarthen Bay and surrounded by woodland. Calm, country house décor and atmosphere and individual rooms. Candlelit dinners in dining room which is decorated in the country style of the establishment.

USK
Glen-yr-Afon House, Pontypool Rd, NP15 1SY, ☎ (01291) 672302; enquiries@glen-yr-afon.co.uk – £74-£94. Across the bridge from the town is this warmly run 19C villa with a relaxing country house ambience. Several welcoming lounges and comfortable, warm, well-kept bedrooms.

WOLF'S CASTLE
Wolfscastle Country Hotel, SA62 5LZ, ☎ (01437) 741225; enquiries@w olfscastle.com – £55-£106. Spacious, family run country house; tidy rooms in traditional soft chintz, modern conference room and simply styled bar with a mix of cushioned settles and old wooden chairs Dining room with neatly laid tables in pink linens.

■ Restaurants ■

The two prices given for each establishment represent a minimum and maximum price for a full meal excluding beverages.

ABERAERON
Harbour Master, Quay Parade, SA46 0BA, ☎ (01545) 570755; info@harbour-master.com – £22-£28. Good value, former harbour master's house, located on attractive quayside. Stylish décor throughout and run in a relaxing style. Snug bar; individually styled bedrooms (£50-£100). Nautically themed dining room with a seafood grounding.

ABERGAVENNY
The Walnut Tree Inn, Llandewi Skirrid, NP7 8AW, ☎ (01873) 852797; francesco@thewalnuttreeinn.com – £18-£42. Renowned inn displays work by Welsh artists. Rustic Italian cooking, full-flavoured and seasonal, local produce: book ahead. Good-value lunch menu.

The Foxhunter, Nant-y-Derry, NP7 9DN, ☎ (01873) 881101; lisatebbutt@aol.com – £22 £23 £34. Bright, contemporary feel within flint-stone former 19C ticket master's office. Light and airy in summer and cosy in the winter. Modern menus using fine local ingredients.

BRECON
Felin Fach Griffin, Felin Fach, LD3 0UB, ☎ (01874) 620111; enquiries @eatdrinksleep.ltd.uk – £20-£27. Terracotta hued traditional pub, once a farmhouse. Characterful interior boasts log fire with sofas, antiques and reclaimed furniture. Modern menus and smart bedrooms (£58-£116).

The White Swan, Llanfrynach, LD3 7BZ, ☎ (01874) 665276; – £17-£25. Characterful village pub: open fires, brick and beams, cheerful service, real ales and a modern and classic menu: from chicken broth to pannacotta and balsamic strawberries.

Usk Inn, Talybont-on-Usk, LD3 7JE, ☎ (01874) 676251; stay@uskinn.co.uk – £10-£31. Country pub near the River Usk. Open fires in the spacious comfy sitting room. Large dining room serving seasonal dishes. Well-kept bedrooms (£45-£90).

BRIDGEND
Frolics, Beach Rd, Southerndown, CF32 0RP, ☎ (01656) 880127; sandmartfrolics@aol.com – £18-£29. Personally run restaurant named after 17C ship wrecked on nearby coast. Cosy neighbourhood style. Excellent menus make full use of area's abundance of fresh fish and seafood.

Leicester's, High St, Laleston, CF32 0HP, ☎ (01656) 657644; enquiries@great-house-laleston.co.uk – £29-£38. Peppermint green walls with exposed beams, fireplace and original windows. Imaginative modern style using finest local and Welsh produce. Black beef and lamb recommended.

CAERSWS

Talkhouse, Pontdolgoch, SY17 5JE,✆ (01686) 688919; info@talkhouse.co.uk
– £22-£26. 17C coaching inn on Aberystwyth-Shrewsbury road. Ornate
rustic bar. Dining room opening onto terrace and gardens. Wide ranging
locally-based menu. Stylish well-kept bedrooms (£70-£95).

CARDIFF

Woods Brasserie, The Pilotage Building, Stuart St, Cardiff Bay, CF10 5BW,
✆ **(029) 2049 2400** – £21-£32. Modern brasserie dishes and seafood specials from an open kitchen. Professionally run. Live evening music. Bay view
from the first-floor terrace.

Da Venditto, 7-8 Park Pl, CF10 3DP, ✆ (029) 2023 0781;
toni@vendittogroup.co.uk – £18-£33. Italian restaurant in the basement
of a town house. Stylish contemporary interior with wood floors and
modern furnishings. Well-prepared, seasonal cuisine.

Le Gallois, 6-10 Romilly Cres, CF11 9NR, ✆ (029) 2034 1264;
info@legallois-ycymro.com – £18-£45. Bright and relaxed restaurant
where keen owners provide both friendly service and assured modern
European cooking. Daily changing set price lunch menu available.

Da Castaldo, 5 Romilly Crescent, CF11 9NP, ✆ **(029)** 2022 1905 – £13-
£26. Appealingly modern ambience in a residential setting; jolly owners
add to the relaxed air. Tasty Italian influences enhance the classical cooking.
Good value lunch.

Pearl of the Orient, 1st Floor (Unit U13), Mermaid Quay, Stuart St,
Cardiff Bay, CF10 5BZ, ✆ **(029)** 2049 8080; admin@thepearloftheorient.
com – £14-£28. Situated in up-and-coming Bay area; boasts good views.
Etched glass private dining room; nautically influenced bar. Wide-ranging
Chinese menu with strong Canton base.

La Fosse, 9-11 The Hayes, CF10 1AH, ✆ (029) 2023 7755 – £11-£31.
Subterranean restaurant boasting a distinctive feel; former fishmarket
building. Open kitchen with chilled seafood display. Modish menus have an
appealing, wide-ranging base.

Armless Dragon, 97 Wyeverne Rd, CF24 4BJ, ✆ (029) 2038 2357; paul@t
hearmlessdragon.fsnet.co.uk – £10-£34. Well-established, homely restaurant
with welcoming atmosphere and snug décor. Daily changing blackboard
menus feature honest, no-nonsense cooking utilising Welsh ingredients.

Izakaya Japanese Tavern, 1st Floor, Mermaid Quay, Cardiff Bay, CF10 5BN,
✆ (029) 2049 2939; ayakazi@aol.com – £17-£35. Smartly furnished restaurant in bay-side location: banners and paper lanterns predominate. Individual
tables or counter service. Authentic, high quality Japanese menus.

The Old Post Office, Greenwood Lane, St Fagans, CF5 6EL, ✆ (029) 2056
5400; heidioldpost@aol.com – £16-£33. The eponymous building in this pleasant hamlet is now a spacious, rustic restaurant with stylish bar. Modern seasonal dishes with notable quality and balance. Excellent rooms (£65-£75).

CARMARTHEN
Four Seasons, Nantgaredig, SA32 7NY, ✆ (01267) 290238; billfourseaso ns@btconnect.com – £30. Smart restaurant, part of hotel complex, in 30 acres of grounds: comfy rustic bedrooms (£55-£80), pleasant swimming pool. Good choice of country dishes, featuring local smoked produce.

COWBRIDGE
Huddarts, 69 High St, CF71 7AF, ✆ (01446) 774645 – £15-£28. Intimate, family run restaurant located on high street of this ancient market town. Welsh tapestries on wall. Skilfully executed traditional dishes with modern influences.

CRICKHOWELL
The Restaurant, High St, NP2 1BN, ✆ (01873) 810408; bearhotel@aol.com – £20-£31. Charming dining rooms with antiques and curios. Open fire in the bar. Professional service. Wide-ranging menu with classical base using Welsh ingredients; daily specials.

CRICKHOWELL
Nantyffin Cider Mill Inn, Brecon Rd, NP8 1SG, ✆ (01873) 810775; info@cidermill.co.uk – £20-£31. Converted 16C cider mill, its working parts still in situ. Rattan flooring and scrubbed pine tables. Varied menus featuring local fish and game. Also, unsurprisingly, cider.

EAST ABERTHAW
Blue Anchor Inn, CF62 3DD, ✆ (01446) 750329 – £14-£23. Characterful thatched and creeper covered inn, dating back to 1380. Nooks, crannies and warrens invoke charming atmosphere. Wide-ranging menus with creative dishes.

FISHGUARD
Three Main Street, 3 Main St, SA65 9HG, ✆ (01348) 874275 – £30. Well-established restaurant just of the market square. Comfortable antique furnished bedrooms (£50-£80). Makes good use of fresh ingredients, particularly local fish and vegetables.

Stone Hall, Welsh Hook, SA62 5NS, ✆ (01348) 840212 – £23-£29. Charming, characterful part 14C manor house with 17C additions. Tranquil setting and personal hospitality. Offers home-cooked, French-style menu and simple accommodation (£50-£85).

HAY-ON-WYE
The Pear Tree, 6 Church St, HR3 5DQ, ✆ (01497) 820777 – info@peartreeathay.co.uk – £20-£24. Stone-built 18C house on the edge of the second-hand book shop town. Outdoor terrace with umbrellas overlooking the garden. Daily menu using local produce at lunch and dinner.

Old Black Lion, Lion St HR3 5AD, ✆ (01497) 820841 – info@oldblacklion.co.uk – £17-£26. Inn with parts dating back to 13C and 17C when it reputedly hosted Oliver Cromwell. A friendly place with a traditional atmosphere, popular menu and comfortable bedrooms (£50-£85).

LLANFYLLIN

Seeds, 5 Penybryn Cottages, High St SY22 5AP, ☎ (01691) 648604 – £15-£24. Converted 16C rustic cottages with eclectic décor: souvenirs from owner's travels. Blackboard menu offers modern or traditional dishes. Local seasonal ingredients to the fore.

LLANWRTYD WELLS

Carlton House, Dolycoed Rd, LD5 4RA ☎ (01591) 610248 info@carlton restaurant.co.uk – £33-£40. Personally run, Victorian house; unpretentious and relaxing feel. Tasty seasonable dishes made with local ingredients. Comfortable rooms (£50-£80).

MONMOUTH

The Crown at Whitebrook, Whitebrook, NP25 4TX, ☎ (01600) 860254; crown@whitebrook.demon.co.uk – £16-£30. Personally run, with a traditional, relaxing atmosphere; located in an area of outstanding natural beauty close to Usk Valley. Modern, French based dishes; local ingredients.

Stone Mill, Rockfield, NP25 5SN, ☎ (01600) 716273 – £10-£28. Converted 16C stone cider mill with exposed timbers and stone walls. Leather sofa in sitting area. Warm and friendly service. Modern seasonal dishes; good value set menu.

NEWPORT

The Chandlery, 77-78 Lower Dock St, NP20 1EH, ☎ (01633) 256622 – £12-£30. Converted 18C chandler's store by the River Usk. Personally-run spacious split-level restaurant with nautical theme. Wide-ranging menu of freshly prepared dishes; good value.

The Newbridge, Tredunnock, NP15 1LY, ☎ (01633) 451000; thenewbridge @tinyonline.co.uk – £16-£30. Bright, comfy pub idyllically set by bridge overlooking Usk. Modern and classical techniques applied to locally based dishes. Superb contemporary bedrooms (£85-£125) exude immense style.

PEMBROKE

The Stackpole Inn, Jasons Corner, Stackpole, SA71 5DF, ☎ (01646) 672324 – £14-£23. Typical country pub with exposed beams and bunches of dried hops. Simple and unfussy pub good served at well-spaced wooden tables.

RAGLAN

Clytha Arms, NP7 9BW, ☎ (01873) 840206; one.bev@lineone.net – £15-£30. Personally run converted dower house close to Abergavenny. Welcoming, open fires; traditional games sprinkled around bar. Generous menus utilise the best of Welsh produce.

ST DAVIDS

Morgan's Brasserie, 20 Nun St, SA62 6NT, ☎ (01437) 720508 morgans@stdavids.co.uk – £25-£30. Unpretentious place in neat burgundy and white, run by a friendly couple. Classics like pork in Calvados plus tasty daily specials like sole with cockles or fresh lobster.

SKENFRITH

The Bell, NP7 8UH, ☏ (01600) 750235; enquiries@skenfrith.com – £20-£32. 17C coaching inn retains much original charm with antiques and curios and open fires. Very comfortable bedrooms (£70-£150) have state-of-the-art appointments. Daily changing modern menu.

SWANSEA

Didier & Stephanie's, 56 St Helens Rd, SA1 4BE, ☏ (01792) 655603 – £12-£22. Cosy, neighbourhood-styled restaurant with a strong Gallic influence. Welcoming owners provide tasty, good value, seasonally changing menus with lots of French ingredients.

Hanson's, Pilot House Wharf, Trawler Rd, Swansea Marina, SA1 1UN, ☏ (01792) 466200; hans1marina@aol.com – £14-£28. Friendly, easygoing restaurant above a tackle shop and in sight of the harbour. Blackboard fish specials are the pick of a carefully sourced repertoire. Good value lunch.

Claudes, 93 Newton Rd, The Mumbles, SA3 4BN, ☏ (01792) 366006; enquiries@claudes.org.uk – £11-£27. An intimate ambience prevails in this personally run restaurant; vividly coloured prints enhance feel. Tasty, modish menus utilising local produce. Wide-ranging wine list.

The Welcome To Town, Llanrhidian, SA3 1EH, ☏ (01792) 390015; enquiries@thewelcometotown.co.uk – £15-£30. Converted pub set on picturesque peninsula. Rustic, characterful interior. Daily blackboard specials and good service of seasonal dishes cooked with real quality.

TALBOT GREEN

Brookes, 79-81 Talbot Rd, CF72 8AE, ☏ (01443) 239600 – £14-£35. The bright blue canopied entrance sets the tone for this vibrant, modern restaurant in the centre of town. Wide-ranging menu offers an eclectic choice of modern food.

TINTERN

Parva Farmhouse, NP16 6SQ, ☏ (01291) 689411; parva_hoteltintern@hotmail.com – £19-£22. Mid 17C stone farmhouse adjacent to River Wye; refurbished to country standard. Traditional cooking, warm hospitality and a wide-ranging wine list. Comfortable rooms (£55-£78).

■ What to buy locally ■

Craftwork is a living tradition in Wales; in craft centres all over the country skilled men and women demonstrate their talents and sell their products. Many museums also have demonstrations of traditional crafts.

Wales – A Touring Guide to Crafts is published by the Wales Tourist Board; local Tourist Information Centres provide information about their own areas. Other bodies providing information on Welsh crafts are:

Visual Arts and Crafts, Arts Council for Wales, 9 Museum Place, Cardiff CF10 3NX ☎ 029 2037 6500; Fax 029 2022 1447; 29 2039 0027 (minicom); information@ccc-acw.org.uk; www.craftinwales.com

Wales Craft Council, Henfaes Lane Industrial Estate, Henfaes Lane, Welshpool SY21 7BE; ☎ 01938 555 313; Fax 01938 556 237; crefft.cymru @btinternet.com; www.walescraftcouncil.co.uk

The crafts practised include fashion garments, glass-blowing, jewellery, pewter work, pottery, slate work, weaving and wood-turning.

Apart from providing sweet Welsh lamb for the table, the many sheep on the hillsides provide wool which is woven into a variety of **woollen goods** – elegant and fashionable garments for men and women as well as the traditional rugs and blankets. There are mills in most parts of the country.

The **slate** which provides roofs and fences is also made into commemorative plaques and other objects of beauty.

Local glass manufacturers produce **glassware** with typical Welsh designs.

Wooden articles from furniture to a simple salad bowl are hand-turned on the lathe or various types of wood are carved into the elaborate Welsh lovespoons.

Lovespoons
The tradition of carving lovespoons probably dates from the Middle Ages when the spoons were used for eating. They now serve a purely decorative purpose and the handle is highly ornate. The suitor, who fashioned the spoon himself, would spend time and effort to make it elaborate as a measure of his affection. Individual motifs were used to indicate particular intentions: the spoon itself indicated that the suitor would provide for his wife; the wheel that he would work for her; the heart indicated love; the keyhole indicated the provision of a house; the number of links in a chain indicated the number of children hoped for. The maritime symbols – anchors and ships – were probabaly carved by sailors during long sea voyages.

The custom of giving and acceptance of a lovespoon as a symbol of betrothal died out in 19C but in recent years they have again become popular in Wales to commemorate special occasions and among visitors as mementoes of their visit.

■ Recreation ■

Wales is an excellent place for many outdoor sports owing to its long coastline, its many lakes and rivers, and the valleys and hills. Further information on all the activities listed below is available from the Wales Tourist Board *(p 102)* or directly from the organisation concerned.

■ Visiting ■

Historic Properties – Many country houses, gardens, historic monuments and ruins are owned or maintained by the following organisations which offer free admission to their members.

The **Great British Heritage Pass** (valid for 7 days, 15 days or one month), which gives access to over 600 properties (country houses, castles and gardens) throughout Great Britain, is available from BTA Offices and Tourist Information Centres.

CADW – The organisation, whose name means "To protect", manages 131 ancient monuments, including many castles, in all parts of Wales. Visitors who intend to visit more than a small number of CADW properties, should consider becoming members of CADW or of English Heritage, whose members have visiting rights.

CADW: Welsh Historic Monuments, Crown Building, Cathays Park, Cardiff CF10 3NQ. ☏ 029 2050 0200; Fax 029 2082 6375; cadw@wales.gsi.gov.uk; www.cadw.wales.gov.uk

English Heritage: Customer Services Department, PO Box 9019, London, W1A 0JA. ☏ 020 7973 3434; www.english-heritage.org.uk

National Trust – The National Trust owns and conserves places of historic interest and natural beauty, including coast and countryside properties, throughout both Wales and England. Non-members of such organisations should consider joining the National Trust if they intend to visit more than a very small number of the Trust properties.

Head Office: National Trust, 36 Queen Anne's Gate, London SW1H 9AS. ☏ 020 7222 9251; Fax 020 7222 5097; www.nationaltrust.org.uk (for general information about properties and opening times).

North Wales Regional Office: National Trust, Trinity Square, Llandudno, LL30 2DE. ☏ 01492 860 123; Fax 01493 860 233.

National Parks – Wales has three national parks – Snowdonia, the Brecon Beacons and Pembrokeshire Coast – which offer many opportunities for outdoor activities and sports (walking, rambling), and some forests, which are managed with recreation in mind.

Brecon Beacons National Park, 7 Glamorgan Street, Brecon LD3 7DP. ☏ 01874 624 437; Fax 01874 622 574; ☏ 01874 623 366.

Pembrokeshire Coast National Park, Winch Lane, Haverfordwest SA61 1PY. ☏ 01437 764 636; www.pembrokeshirecoast.org.uk

Snowdonia National Park Authority, Penrhyndeudraeth LL48 6LF. ☏ 01766 770 274.

Nature Reserves – Wales has many nature reserves, some with birdwatching centres, both on the coast and inland where great efforts have been made to re-establish the red kite in its native habitat.

RSPB Wales (Royal Society for the Protection of Birds), Sutherland House, Castlebridge, Cowbridge Road East, Cardiff CF11 9AB ☎ 020 2035 3000 Fax 029 2035 3017; www.rspb.org.uk/cymru/defaults.htm

Wildfowl and Wetlands Trust, Canolfan Llanelli Centre, Penclacwydd, Llanelli, Dyfed SA14 9SH. ☎ 01554 741 087; www.wwt.org.uk

Kite Country, Bryn Aderyn, The Bank, Newtown, Powys SY16 2AB. ☎ 01686 624 143.

Council for National Parks, 246 Lavender Hill, London SW11 1LJ. ☎ 020 7924 4077; Fax 020 7924 5761; www.cnp.org.uk

Countryside Council for Wales, Plas Penrhos, Ffordd Penrhos, Bangor LL57 2LQ. ☎ 01248 385 500.

Forestry Enterprise, Victoria House, Victoria Terrace, Aberystwyth SY23 2DQ. ☎ 01970 612 367.

Gardens – The National Gardens Scheme publishes *Gardens of England and Wales*, an annual guide to private gardens which are open to the public for a limited period in aid of charity.

National Gardens Scheme, Hatchlands Park, East Clandon, Guildford, Surrey GU4 7RT. ☎ 01483 211 535; Fax 01483 211 537.

Music – Wales has a long tradition and widespread reputation for music, particularly the human voice, and poetry.

The **Welsh Male Voice Choirs**, of which there are over 60, usually admit members of the public to their rehearsals. A booklet giving rehearsal locations and times, and the names, addresses and telephone numbers of contacts – *Welsh Male Voice Choirs (Corau Meibion Cymru)* – is available from the Wales Tourist Board *(see p 102)* or from local Tourist Information Centres.

The **International Musical Eisteddfod**, held in Llangollen annually in early July (5 days), offers performances by male voice choirs, female choirs, mixed choirs, folk song groups, children's choirs, solo singers and of opera.

International Musical Eisteddfod Office, First Floor, Royal International Pavilion, Abbey Road, Llangollen LL20 8FW. ☎ 01978 862 000, Fax 01978 862 002; tickets@international-eisteddfod.co.uk; www.international-eisteddfod.co.uk

The **National Eisteddfod of Wales**, which is held annually in August (9 days), in North Wales and South Wales in alternate years, promotes the Welsh language through a Welsh cultural fair; Welsh dancing, music and poetry recitations in the Bardic tradition take place in the Main Pavilion, while the satellites provide concerts, plays, arts and crafts and science exhibitions.

National Eisteddfod of Wales, 40 Parc Ty Glas, Llanishen, Cardiff CF14 5WU. ☎ 029 2076 3777; Fax 029 2076 3737; info@eisteddfod.org.uk; www.eisteddfod.org.uk

■ Sport ■

Rambling – Wales is a walker's paradise, with a dense network of rights of way and exhilarating mountain and coastal paths. There are two national trails and several waymarked long-distance routes. There are also many trails in nature reserves and forests.

Ramblers in Wales, Tŷ'r Cerddwyr, High Street, Gresford, Wrexham LL12 8PT. ☎ 01978 855 148, Fax 01978 854 445; cerddwyr@wales.ramblers.org .uk; www.ramblers.org.uk

Ramblers' Association, 2nd floor, Camelford, 87-90 Albert Embankment, London SE1 7TW. ☎ 020 7339 8500; Fax 0171 7339 8501; www.ramblers.org.uk

Offa's Dyke Footpath – This national trail *(177mi/285m)* runs along the English border from its northern end near Prestatyn to its southern end at Sedbury Cliffs on the River Severn just east of Chepstow; there are information centres in Prestatyn and Knighton.

Offa's Dyke Association, West Street, Knighton, Powys. ☎ 01547 528 753.

Glyn Dŵr Way – This path (128mi/206km – 8 to 12 days) makes a loop through mid-Wales from Knighton west via Abbey-cym-hir, Llanidloes, Clywedog Reservoir to Machynlleth, returning east via Llanbrynmair, Llangadfan, Lake Vyrnwy and Maifod to Welshpool. It is designed as a walking route and is therefore not available for use as a bridle or cycle route; it includes long stretches across agricultural land, where dogs must be kept on a lead. The current route was established by Powys County Council during the mid-1970s and is currently managed by Powys County Council in partnership with the Countryside Council for Wales; maintenance work is carried out by landowners, volunteers and contractors. There are railway stations at Knighton and Llangunllo on the Heart of Wales Line and at Machynlleth and Welshpool on the Cambrian Line. There are bus services linking Llanidloes, Machynlleth and Welshpool, and a limited bus service in the rural areas. Brochure available from Machynlleth TIC.

Wye Valley Walk – This path runs beside the river, which, in its lower reaches before it flows into the Severn Estuary, forms the boundary between Wales and England.

Pembrokeshire Coast Path – This national trail gives access to the cliffs and beaches of the Pembrokeshire Coast National Park *(see p 80)*.

Taff Trail – This path, which doubles as a cycle route, runs from Brecon to Cardiff *(55mi/88km)* along the course of the River Taff, using canal towpaths, disused railways and tram roads to provide a safe and scenic route, which has links with a network of cycle routes, circular walks, bridleways, drives and picnic sites. Information booklet available from the Tourist Information Centre in Cardiff *(see p 40)*.

Pilgrims' Road – This path runs along the north coast of the Lleyn Peninsula from Bangor to Aberdaron. Pilgrims set out from Bangor Cathedral and proceeded along the coast to Aberdaron, where they embarked in a boat to cross Bardsey Sound to reach their goal, the monastery on Bardsey Island. As they walked they stopped to pray and worship at some or all of the other 11 churches along the route – Caernarfon, Llanwnda, Llandwrog, Clynnog Fawr, Llanaelhaearn, Pistyll, Nefyn, Edern, Tudweiliog, Penllech and Llangwnnadl.

Coed Morgannwg Way – This footpath (32mi/52km) runs from Margam Country Park on the shore of Swansea Bay to the Craig-y-Llyn viewpoint beyond the head of the Rhondda Valley.

Mountain Biking and Climbing – Centres for hiring and using mountain bikes and quad bikes are fairly numerous.

Snowdonia in North Wales is one of the cradles of British mountaineering where serious climbers spend time in training for their attempts at greater things, such as the conquest of Everest. The Brecon Beacons *(see p 30)* also provide a challenge.

Mountain walkers should bear in mind that temperatures drop rapidly as height is gained, roughly by 2 C for every 1 000ft/300m. This, combined with wind-chill, means that summit conditions can be unpleasantly, even dangerously, different from those which seemed so encouraging at the starting point of a climb in the valley bottom.

National Mountaineering Centre, Plas y Brenin, Capel Curig. ☎ 01690 720 214; Fax 01690 720 394; info@pyb.co.uk; www.pyb.co.uk

British Mountaineering Council, 177-179 Burton Road, West Didsbury, Manchester, M20 2BB. ☎ 0161 445 4747; Fax 0161 445 4500; www.thebmc.co.uk

Golf – Details of the more than 160 golf courses in Wales are given in the Wales Tourist Board's comprehensive brochure *Golfing in Wales*. Many are listed in the **Michelin Red Guide Great Britain and Ireland**. Most are privately owned and accept visitors. Municipal courses are usually very heavily used, with long queues at the first tee.

Royal and Ancient Golf Club of St Andrews, St Andrews, Fife KY16 9JD. ☎ 01334 472 112; Fax 01334 477 580;www.randa.org

English Golf Union, National Golf Centre, The Broadway, Woodhall Spa, Lincolnshire LN10 6PU. ☎ 01526 354 500; Fax 01526 354 020; www.englishgolfunion.org

English Ladies Golf Association, Edgbaston Golf Club, Church Road, Birmingham B15 3TB. ☎ 0121 456 2088; Fax 0121 454 5542; office@engl ishladiesgolf.org

Cycling – Much of Wales is ideal mountain biking country, and there are also combined cycling and walking routes like the Taff Trail leading north from Cardiff into the South Wales Valleys. A Cycle Network is being established so that Wales can be crossed by bicycle from north to south and east to west; these routes are part of the National Cycle Network covering the whole of Britain comprising 5 000mi/8 000km of traffic-free routes and traffic-calmed and minor roads. For information apply to

SUSTRANS, Head Office, 35 King Street, Bristol BS1 4DZ. ☎ 0117 926 8893; 0117 929 0888 (information line); Fax 0117 929 4173; www.sustrans.co.uk

Cycles are available for hire from a number of centres. The Wales Tourist Board brochure *Cycling Wales* gives full details.

Fishing – Wales offers fishing in the lakes and reservoirs and along the coast. There is also the possibility of deep-sea fishing from a limited number of harbours. The Wye and Usk are famous for salmon fishing; Llyn Brenig is preserved exclusively for fly-fishing.

A leaflet on fishing the reservoirs of Wales, giving information on dates, times, permits, charges and facilities for the disabled, is published by the Welsh Water Authority.

Welsh Water Authority, Plas-y-Ffynnon, Cambrian Way, Brecon LD3 7HP. ☎ 01874 623 181, 0800 052 0138 (publications hotline); Fax 01874 624 167; www.hyder.com

National Federation of Anglers, Halliday House, Eggington Junction, Derbyshire DE65 6GU. ☎ 01283 734 735; Fax 01283 734 799; www.the-nfa.org.uk

National Federation of Sea Anglers, 51a Queen Street, Newton Abbot, Devon TQ12 2QJ, ☎/Fax 01626 334 924; nfsaho@aol.com

Salmon and Trout Association, Fishmongers Hall, London Bridge, London EC4R 9EL. ☎ 020 7283 5838; Fax 020 7626 5137; www.salmon-trout.org

Sailing – There are many opportunities for sailing at sea off the long and varied coastline of Wales, in the many estuaries and inland on the lakes and reservoirs (dinghy sailing on Bala Lake and Llangorse Lake). Some of the best sailing is to be found off the Lleyn Peninsula.

Welsh Yachting Association, 8 Llys y Môr, Plas Menai, Llanfairisgair, Caernarfon, LL55 1UE. ☎ 01248 670 738 (9.30-11.30am); www.thewya.fr eeserve.co.uk

Canoeing – Canoeing on Welsh rivers can include white-water experience. Llandysul on the River Teifi, upstream of Newcastle Emlyn, is a popular venue for the National Canoeing Championships. Canoeists also favour the beaches in St Bride's Bay.

Welsh Canoeing Association, Canolfan Tryweryn, Frongoch, Bala LL23 7NU. ☎ 01678 521 199; Fax 01678 521 158; welsh.canoeing@virgin .net; www.welsh-canoeing.org.uk

Surfing – Surfing is popular on a number of west-facing beaches, particularly those in St Bride's Bay and on the Lleyn Peninsula.

Welsh Surfing Federation, 29 Sterry Road, Gowerton, Swansea SA4 3BS. ☎ 01729 529 898; Fax 01792 529 897; wsf@ntl.com

Riding and pony trekking – This well-developed activity is fully described in the Wales Tourist Board brochure *Discovering Wales on Horseback*.

Wales Trekking and Riding Association, 7 Rhosferig Road, Brecon LD3 7NG. ☎ 01874 623 185; Fax 01874 623 775; info@totaltourism.co.uk; www.ridingwales.com

Horseracing – There are few racecourses in Wales itself but Chester and Cheltenham are only a short distance over the border in England.

The **flat racing** season at Chepstow runs from late May to mid-September. There is steeplechasing at Chepstow from early October to May and at Bangor-on-Dee from February to May and August to December.

Chepstow Racecourse, Chepstow NP16 6BE. ☎ 01291 622 260; Fax 01921 627 061; info@chepstow-racecourse.co.uk; www.chepstow-racecourse.co.uk

■ Further reading ■

For reference...

Wild Wales by George Borrow (Bridge, 2002)

A Pocket Modern Welsh Dictionary: A Guide to the Living Language by Janet Davies (University of Wales Press, 2000)

A History of Wales by John Davies (Penguin, 1994)

The Revolt of Owain Glyn Dwr by RR Davies (Oxford University Press, 2001)

Wales in the Early Middle Ages by Wendy Davies (Leicester University Press, 1982)

Modern Wales: A Concise History, 1485-1979 by Gareth Elwyn Jones (Cambridge University Press, 1984)

Getting Yesterday Right: Interpreting the History of Wales by J Geraint Jenkins (University of Wales Press, 1992)

Historic Architecture of Wales by John B Hilling (University of Wales Press, 1976)

A History of Modern Wales 1536-1990 by Philip Jenkins (Longman, 1991)

Welsh Chapels by Anthony Jones (Sutton Publishing, 1997)

Modern Welsh: A Comprehensive Grammar by Gareth King (Routledge, 2002)

Wales 1880-1980 Rebirth of a Nation by Kenneth O Morgan (Oxford University Press, 1982)

The Matter of Wales: Epic Views of a Small Country by Jan Morris (Penguin, 1986)

Wales from the Air by Jan Morris (Ebury, 2001)

The National Museum of Wales Companion Guide by Timothy Stevens (National Museum of Wales, 1993)

Wales: An Anthology ed by Alice Thomas Ellis (Fontana, 1991)

When Was Wales?: A History of the Welsh by Gwyn A Williams (Penguin, 1985)

For pleasure...

On the Black Hill by Bruce Chatwin (Vintage, 1998)

The Mabinogion translated by Gwyn and Thomas Jones (Everyman, 2001)

How Green Was My Valley by Richard Llewellyn (Penguin, 2001)

Dylan: Fern Hill to Milk Wood by David Rowe (Gomer Press, 1999)

Collected Stories by Dylan Thomas (Phoenix, 2000)

Clouds of Time and other stories by John E Williams (Gwasg Carreg Gwalch, 1999)

■ Calendar of events ■

1 March
Throughout Wales   St David's Day: celebrated all over the country, with special services in St David's Cathedral

1 May
St Fagan's   May Day celebrations at the Museum of Welsh Life, St Fagan's, near Cardiff

Late May-end December
Throughout Wales   Mid-Wales festival of the Countryside – over 500 events such as birdwatching, guided walks, arts and crafts, sheepdog trials, farm and garden visits

Late May-early June
Hay-on-Wye   Hay Festival of Literature and the Arts

Late May-early June
Variable location   The Urdd National (Welsh League of Youth) Eisteddfod, one of the largest youth festivals in Europe

Early August
Variable location   Royal National Eisteddfod of Wales (9 days)

Mid-August (3 days)
Brecon   Brecon Jazz Festival – international festival attracting the top names from the world of jazz

Late August (1 week)
Llandrindod Wells   Llandrindod Wells Victorian Festival – street theatre, drama, exhibitions, walks, talks and music – all with a Victorian flavour

Last full week of August
Machynlleth   Arts Festival

Late September
Tenby   Tenby Arts Festival

Late September-early October
Cardiff   Cardiff Festival

October
Swansea   Swansea Festival of Music and the Arts

INDEX

G

H

I - K

L

M

Director	David Brabis
Series Editor	Mike Brammer
Editor	Alison Hughes
Picture Editor	Eliane Bailly, Geneviève Corbic
Mapping	Michèle Cana, Alain Baldet
Graphics Coordination	Marie-Pierre Renier
Graphics	Antoine Diemoz-Rosset
Lay-out	Alain Fossé
Typesetting	Sophie Rassel and Franck Malagie (NORDCOMPO)
Production	Renaud Leblanc
Marketing	Cécile Petiau, Hervé Binétruy
Sales	John Lewis (UK), Robin Bird (USA)
Public Relations	Gonzague de Jarnac, Paul Cordle
Contact	Michelin Travel Publications
	Hannay House
	39 Clarendon Road
	Watford
	Herts
	WD17 1JA
	United Kingdom
	☎ (01923) 205 240
	Fax (01923) 205 241
	www.ViaMichelin.com
	TheGreenGuide-uk@uk.michelin.com

Travel Publications

Hannay House, 39 Clarendon Road.
Watford, Herts WD17 1JA, UK
www.ViaMichelin.com
TheGreenGuide-uk@uk.michelin.com

. . . .

MANUFACTURE FRANÇAISE DES PNEUMATIQUES MICHELIN
Société en commandite par actions au capital de 304 000 000 EUR
Place des Carmes-Déchaux – 63 Clermont-Ferrand (France)
R.C.S. Clermont-Fd B 855 200 507

Published in 2004